RYA Day Skipper Handbook – Sail
by Sara Hopkinson

Illustrator: Pete Galvin

© Sara Hopkinson / RYA 2012
First Published 2012
Reprinted October 2013, May 2015

The Royal Yachting Association
RYA House, Ensign Way, Hamble,
Southampton SO31 4YA
Tel: 0844 556 9555
Fax: 0844 556 9516
E-mail: publications@rya.org.uk
Web: www.rya.org.uk
Follow us on Twitter @RYAPublications or
on YouTube
ISBN: 9781-9051-04949
RYA Order Code: G71

A CIP record of this book is available from the British Library.

Note: While all reasonable care had been taken in the preparation of this book, the publisher takes no responsibility for the use of the methods or products or contracts described in the book.

Cover Design: Pete Galvin
Typesetting and Design: Velveo Design
Proofreading and indexing: Alan Thatcher
Cover photograph: tallshipstock.com
Printed in China through World Print

Contents

Foreword

Skippering a cruising yacht can be a very rewarding activity. You have the freedom to more or less go where you choose and have the satisfaction of a job well done when you get your yacht and crew safely to their destination.

The Day Skipper practical course is one of the most important courses in the RYA Yachtmaster Scheme. It puts the foundations in place for safe and enjoyable skippering, ensuring you and your crew get the most out of your sailing.

Whether you are looking to gain more confidence to go on charter holidays, with no intention of going beyond Day Skipper, or are at the beginning of a grand plan to skipper large superyachts, you will reach your goal quicker and with more enjoyment if you start with a solid grounding in the skippering techniques and practical skills required.

This book covers the content of the Day Skipper practical course in enough detail to help as a pre-course read or as a reference text during and after your course. It is full of top tips based on many hours of skippering and instructing within the RYA Yachtmaster Scheme. I hope you find it useful in progressing your sailing towards your goal.

Happy sailing!

Vaughan Marsh

RYA Chief Instructor,
Sail Cruising

Introduction

Becoming an RYA Day Skipper is an important and exciting step. It brings together the sailing experience of the RYA Competent Crew Course and the RYA Day Skipper Practical Course as well as the theory part of the RYA Day Skipper Shorebased Course. Add to this the experience of sailing on a variety of boats and you are well on your way to become a safe and confident skipper taking your family and friends on enjoyable cruising holidays.

Being a good skipper is not difficult; it requires essential skills, knowledge, experience, patience, good communication and at times a sense of humour! Look at how easy experienced skippers often make very difficult situations appear. Essential skills include; applying the Collision Regulations (Colregs), keeping a good lookout at all times, knowledge of the weather forecast and sailing area you intend to sail in, what safety kit to carry, when and how to use it, how to deal with gear failure repairs and being able to do this all at the same time as keeping your boat, self and crew safe and happy.

It's a bit like juggling. Tossing and catching one ball is easy, some people can do two, but it is only the skilled who achieve three or more after having learned and practised their skills over many years.

Sounds daunting? The good news is, most of the time you will not be alone on the boat, you will have crew. However some skippers insist on trying to do everything themselves – an impossible feat. They then wonder why the crew are bored or even scared. Taking a team approach makes a cruise stress free, interesting and enjoyable for all onboard. Ensuring the crew know what they must do and how to do it makes sailing safer and more enjoyable for all.

1 Nautical Terms

List of Common Sailing Terms

Bear away: Turn away from the wind.

Cleat: A stationary device used to secure a rope aboard a boat.

Dodger: A hood forward of a hatch or to the side of a cockpit to protect the crew from wind and spray.

DSC: Digital Selective Calling

Fairlead: A ring or hook used to keep a line running in the correct direction or to prevent it fouling.

Flaking: Lay out a rope or chain in loose coils to prevent it tangling.

Fractional rig: A foresail that does not reach the top of the mast.

Halyard: Line used to raise the head (top) of a sail.

Head up: Change direction to point closer to the wind.

MMSI: Maritime Mobile Service Identity

Overfall: Steep and breaking sea due to opposing currents and wind in a shallow area, or strong currents over a shallow rocky seabed.

Preventer: Sail control line originating at some point on the boom leading to a fixed point on the boat's deck or rail to prevent or moderate the effects of an accidental jibe.

Propwalk: The tendency for a propeller, when rotating, to push the stern sideways.

Ram's horn: Hook attached to the gooseneck to aid mainsail reefing.

Reef: Temporarily reduce the area of a sail exposed to the wind.

Roller furling: Method of furling or reefing by rolling a sail around a stay or rotating spar.

Shrouds: Pieces of rigging that hold the mast up.

Spreader: A spar used to deflect the shrouds to allow them to support the mast.

Warp: Rope or cable used when moving a boat in a confined space.

Wind indicator: Swiveling device used to determine the direction of the wind in relation to the boat's heading.

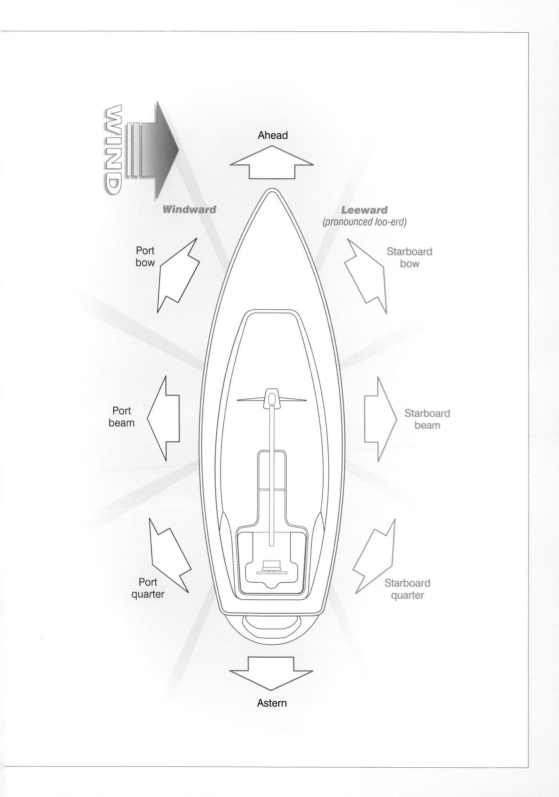

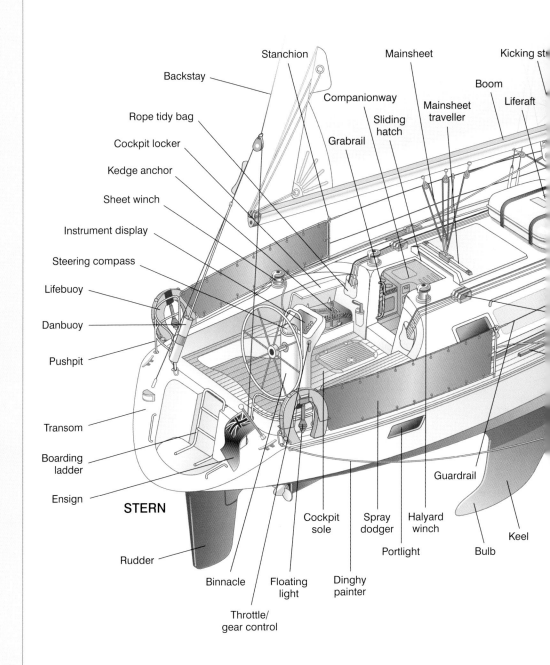

Stanchion

Mainsheet

Kicking st

Backstay

Companionway

Boom

Rope tidy bag

Sliding
hatch

Mainsheet
traveller

Liferaft

Cockpit locker

Grabrail

Kedge anchor

Sheet winch

Instrument display

Steering compass

Lifebuoy

Danbuoy

Pushpit

Transom

Boarding
ladder

Guardrail

Ensign

STERN

Cockpit
sole

Spray
dodger

Halyard
winch

Keel

Rudder

Portlight

Bulb

Binnacle

Floating
light

Dinghy
painter

Throttle/
gear control

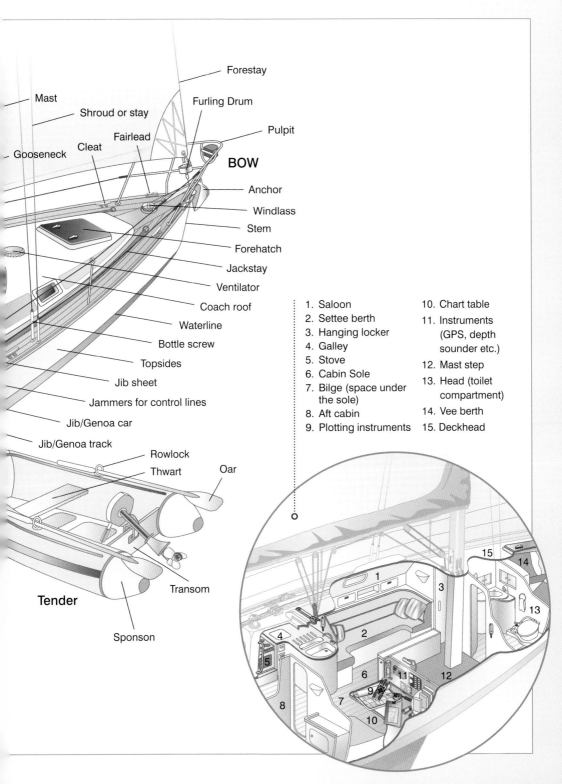

Mast

Shroud or stay

Forestay

Furling Drum

Fairlead

Cleat

Pulpit

Gooseneck

BOW

Anchor

Windlass

Stem

Forehatch

Jackstay

Ventilator

Coach roof

Waterline

Bottle screw

Topsides

Jib sheet

Jammers for control lines

Jib/Genoa car

Jib/Genoa track

Rowlock

Thwart

Oar

Transom

Tender

Sponson

1. Saloon
2. Settee berth
3. Hanging locker
4. Galley
5. Stove
6. Cabin Sole
7. Bilge (space under the sole)
8. Aft cabin
9. Plotting instruments
10. Chart table
11. Instruments (GPS, depth sounder etc.)
12. Mast step
13. Head (toilet compartment)
14. Vee berth
15. Deckhead

Preparation for Sea

Prepare the vessel for sea before leaving harbour. Brief the crew about the passage and consider the crew's strengths.

Crew

- Give a safety brief.
- Ensure they know the location and how to use all safety equipment.
- Brief the crew about the passage and delegate tasks.
- Check if any crew have a medical condition you should be aware of.
- Check that all have lifejackets that are correctly adjusted. Carry harnesses for deck work.
- If any crew get seasick, make sure they have taken medication.

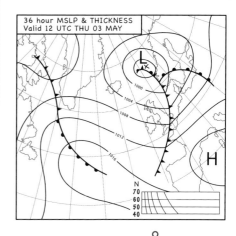

36 hour MSLP & THICKNESS
Valid 12 UTC THU 03 MAY

Weather

- Obtain a weather forecast; if on a longer passage, monitor the weather in the days leading up to the trip. If in a tidal area, find out tidal direction.

Fuel

- Check there is sufficient fuel.

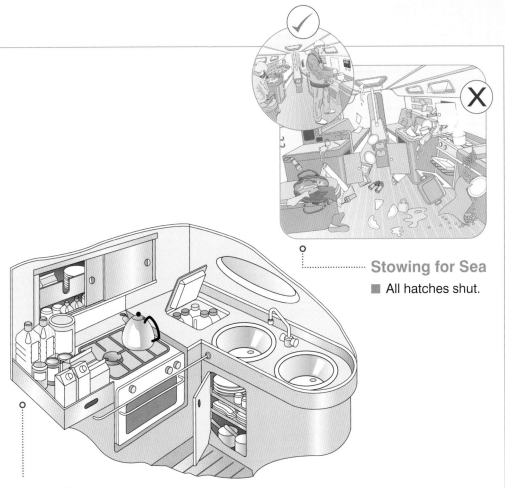

Stowing for Sea

■ All hatches shut.

Victualling

■ Ensure there is enough food and drinks for the voyage.

■ Prepare food in advance as it is very difficult to cook en-route on smaller boats.

■ Stow provisions in dry readily accessible places.

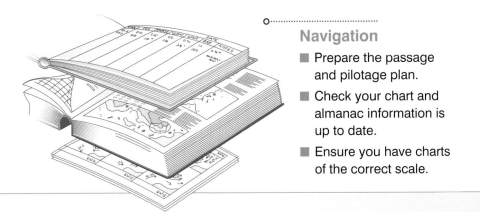

Navigation

■ Prepare the passage and pilotage plan.

■ Check your chart and almanac information is up to date.

■ Ensure you have charts of the correct scale.

Daily Engine Checks

Check for:

1. Oil, fuel or water leaks
2. Low engine oil level and signs of water in the oil
3. Signs of wear or lack of tension on drive belts
4. Water in the water separator
5. Weed or other debris in the water filter
6. Open seacock

1. Remember to check the gearbox oil once a month.
2. Carry simple spares: oil, drive belt, impeller, oil filter and an engine manual and sufficient tools.
3. Keep the fuel tanks topped up to minimise condensation in the tank, especially over the winter. If the level gets low, sediment from the bottom of the tank can be sucked up and block the filters.

After starting the engine always check the following and keep checking them while out on the water.

- The cooling water is coming out.
- The battery is charging.
- Gauges are working correctly.
- Know the sound of your engine and listen for any change as this is often the first sign of an impending problem.

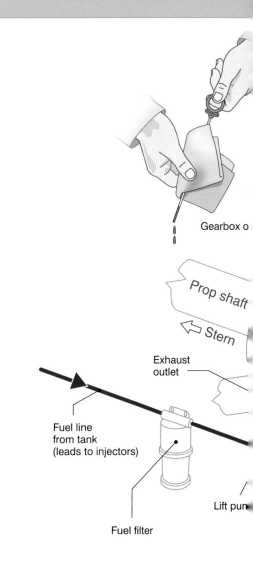

Gearbox o

Prop shaft

Stern

Exhaust outlet

Fuel line from tank (leads to injectors)

Lift pun

Fuel filter

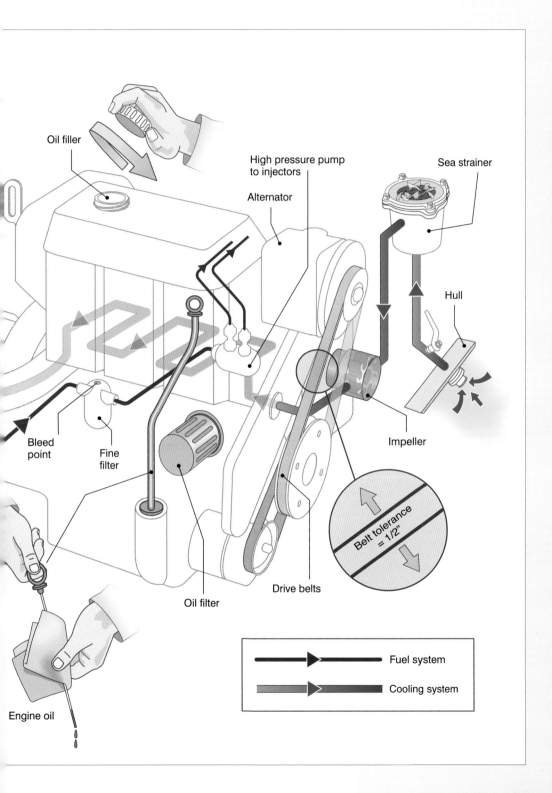

Oil filler

High pressure pump
to injectors

Sea strainer

Alternator

Hull

Bleed
point

Fine
filter

Impeller

Belt tolerance
= 1/2"

Oil filter

Drive belts

Engine oil

Fuel system

Cooling system

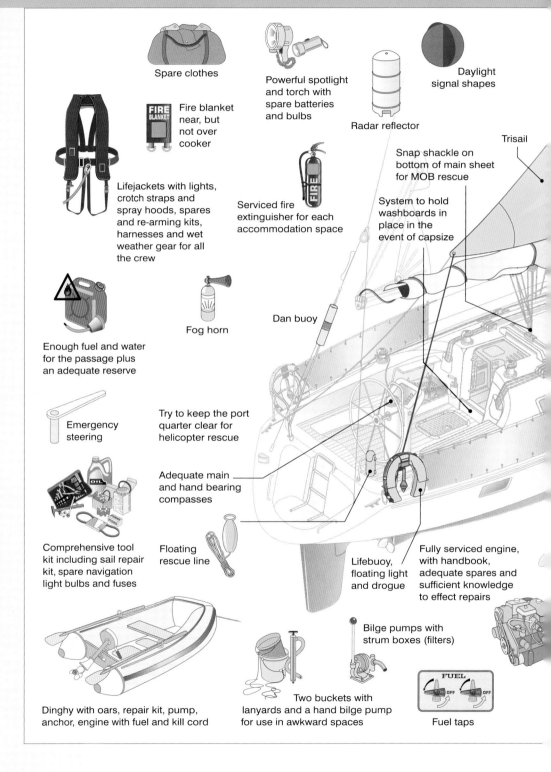

Spare clothes

Powerful spotlight and torch with spare batteries and bulbs

Daylight signal shapes

Fire blanket near, but not over cooker

Radar reflector

Trisail

Lifejackets with lights, crotch straps and spray hoods, spares and re-arming kits, harnesses and wet weather gear for all the crew

Serviced fire extinguisher for each accommodation space

Snap shackle on bottom of main sheet for MOB rescue

System to hold washboards in place in the event of capsize

Fog horn

Dan buoy

Enough fuel and water for the passage plus an adequate reserve

Emergency steering

Try to keep the port quarter clear for helicopter rescue

Adequate main and hand bearing compasses

Comprehensive tool kit including sail repair kit, spare navigation light bulbs and fuses

Floating rescue line

Lifebuoy, floating light and drogue

Fully serviced engine, with handbook, adequate spares and sufficient knowledge to effect repairs

Bilge pumps with strum boxes (filters)

Dinghy with oars, repair kit, pump, anchor, engine with fuel and kill cord

Two buckets with lanyards and a hand bilge pump for use in awkward spaces

FUEL

Fuel taps

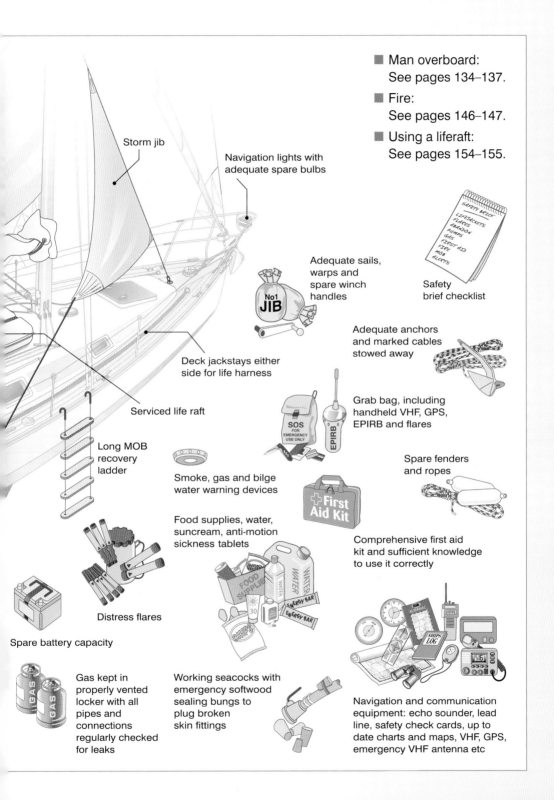

- Man overboard:
  See pages 134–137.
- Fire:
  See pages 146–147.
- Using a liferaft:
  See pages 154–155.

Storm jib

Navigation lights with
adequate spare bulbs

Adequate sails,
warps and
spare winch
handles

Safety
brief checklist

Adequate anchors
and marked cables
stowed away

Deck jackstays either
side for life harness

Grab bag, including
handheld VHF, GPS,
EPIRB and flares

Serviced life raft

Long MOB
recovery
ladder

Smoke, gas and bilge
water warning devices

Spare fenders
and ropes

Food supplies, water,
suncream, anti-motion
sickness tablets

Comprehensive first aid
kit and sufficient knowledge
to use it correctly

Distress flares

Spare battery capacity

Gas kept in
properly vented
locker with all
pipes and
connections
regularly checked
for leaks

Working seacocks with
emergency softwood
sealing bungs to
plug broken
skin fittings

Navigation and communication
equipment: echo sounder, lead
line, safety check cards, up to
date charts and maps, VHF, GPS,
emergency VHF antenna etc

How the Boat Turns and Steers under Power

Good boat handling skills are fundamental to sailing and once learnt and practised are achievable by anyone. This section will help you understand and attain these core skills.

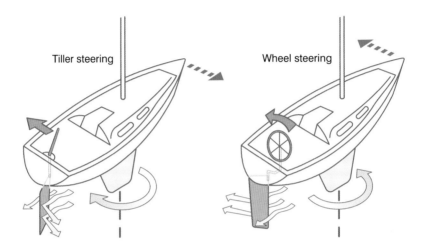

Tiller steering

Wheel steering

As the boat is sailing or motoring along, small movements of the wheel or the tiller alter the angle of the rudder and the angle at which the water is deflected, and the boat changes direction. The best way to learn to steer is by watching the left and right movement of the bows, rather than thinking too much about how far the tiller or wheel has been moved. In normal situations, when the desire is to go straight, the movements should be quite small. Keeping the rudder at a sharp angle or moving it excessively acts as a brake by deflecting more water than necessary.

A tiller may seem to be less straightforward than a wheel, but it has the advantage of showing the angle of the rudder directly.

The steering effect of the rudder can be felt even when the boat is stationary on a mooring if there is water flowing past from a tidal stream or river current. Moving the rudder will change the heading of the boat as the tidal stream is deflected. This is why the wheel or tiller is normally fixed when on a mooring or at anchor.

No water moving past the rudder means no ability to steer.

When manoeuvring under power, consider the basic characteristics of the boat and the external influences on it.

The basic factors of steering a boat:

- The rotation and position of the propeller
- The pivot points as the boat turns in ahead and reverse
- The shape of the boat, the keel length and the height of the superstructure
- Speed. Remember, no water moving past the rudder means no ability to steer

Additional influences to think about, especially when the boat is manoeuvring at slow speed, include:

- Wind
- Tidal stream or river current

Forward and Astern under Power

When steering straight the propeller provides a flow of water over the rudder.

However, on a yacht where the propeller is near the rudder a burst of forward power can be directed against the side of the rudder by turning the rudder hard over, before applying power. This gives a far greater turning effect as the rudder acts as a brake to forward movement and the burst of power is directed against the almost flat side of the rudder. This is useful when manoeuvring in small spaces.

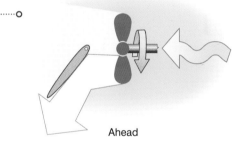

Ahead

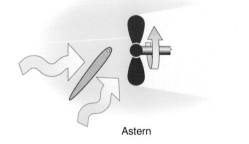

Astern

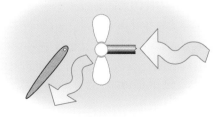

Neutral

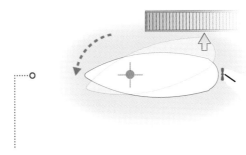

When turning in forward the pivot point will be near the mast, so watch the stern does not come too close to other boats or the corner of a pontoon.

In astern everything is different. The flow of the water from the propeller is away from the rudder, so the boat can be steered only when it begins to move backwards. The rudder is also leading the way, so if it is turned too far or if the boat moves too fast the tiller or wheel will snatch violently, damaging gear or people. Additionally, the pivot point in reverse moves well aft, and the bow can swing wide on a turn.

In reverse:

- Start from stationary, if possible
- Steer holding the tiller or wheel with two hands
- Look over the stern of the boat or even face backwards, but check that the bow is not swinging too much as the pivot point has moved
- Do not go too fast. Use power to get the boat moving, then ease off
- Do not apply too much rudder
- If the direction seems to be going wrong, motor ahead to straighten up and then start again

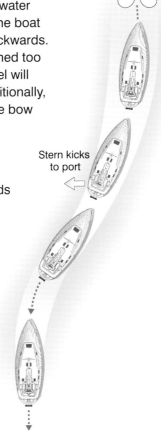

Stern kicks to port

The rotation of the propellers in forward gear may be clockwise (right-handed) or anticlockwise (left-handed) depending on its design. As the water spins off the propeller it creates what is known as propwalk. This sideways pull on the stern can be felt most when reversing, especially when coming out of a marina berth. The propwalk will kick the stern to port or starboard before the boat has enough speed to have steerage way.

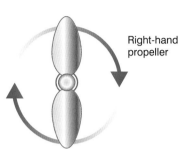

Right-hand propeller

Once the boat is moving, select neutral and the propwalk will disappear. The boat can be steered as long as it has momentum. Being able to predict which way the stern will kick is very important. It can then be used to your advantage in some circumstances, such as coming alongside, or if it will be a problem it can be anticipated.

When going astern, the pivot point moves further aft, so you need to be careful that the bow does not hit other objects such as boats or pontoons.

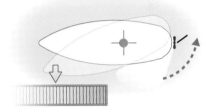

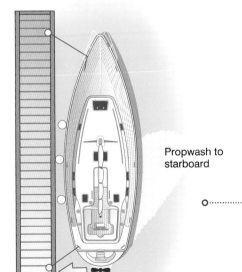

Propwash to starboard

Stern kicks to port

How to Test for Propwalk

In the Marina

When secured alongside, put the engine in reverse. The wash from the propeller should be clearly seen to one side of the stern, and the propwalk will be the other way.

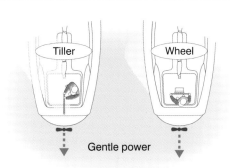

Tiller   Wheel

Gentle power

In Open Water

Start with the boat stern into wind, so there are no other confusing factors involved. Let the boat lose all forward speed. Hold the rudder straight and start reversing. Watch the background over the stern of the boat by lining up the backstay with something on the shore. The stern will kick one way. Once it starts to move backwards, it will steer to the rudder. You may need to use reasonable power to get the boat moving, but then ease up.

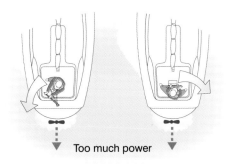

Too much power

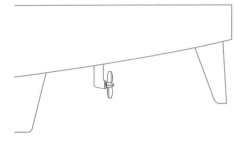

On some yachts the propeller is closer to the keel than to the rudder, producing less propwalk and making a burst of power have less turning effect.

Some propellers fold when not in use to reduce drag and then open with a distinctive "clonk" when the gear is engaged.

With all propellers, as the gear lever is moved from forward to reverse the propeller must stop spinning, then start again in the opposite direction. A brief pause in neutral helps protect the gearbox from damage.

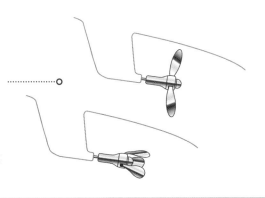

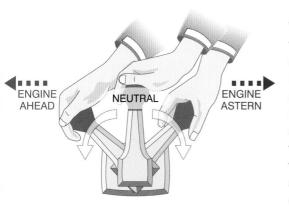

The gear lever is combined with the throttle, so as it is moved the revs and speed will increase. For most boats there is a comfortable cruising speed and highest recommended revs. When manoeuvring, too much speed will increase the size of the turning circle as the boat moves forward during the turn, but too little speed makes the boat vulnerable to external influences, such as wind or tidal stream.

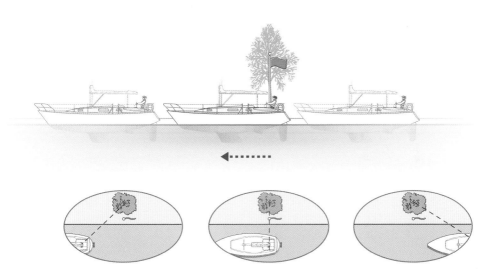

When steering under power, stand so that the throttle is accessible. Assess speed by watching a transit near the beam of the boat, perhaps the mast of another boat against the background.

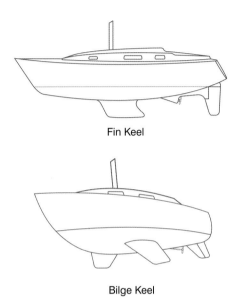

Fin Keel

Long Keel

Bilge Keel

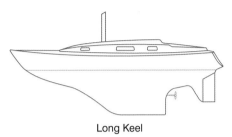

The shape of the boat under the water will affect how well it turns and steers and how much the external influences, wind, tidal stream or river current, affect it.

The sideways effect of the wind, or leeway, will cause the bow of the boat to blow away from the wind. This is especially true at slow speed.

A look at the underwater shape of different yachts shows why some are more affected by leeway than others. A traditional heavy long keel boat will make less leeway than a lighter yacht with a central keel and spade rudder, but the longer keel will make turning more difficult in a small space.

In the marina, look around to assess the strength and direction of the wind. The wind indicator on a motoring boat will show the wind strength and direction modified by its own movement. The Windex® on a stationary boat will give a true picture. Look at flags or even trees to gauge the strength of the wind in a marina. There may be signs on the water too. Even one empty berth on a windy day can produce a gust that can affect the boat. High superstructure, spray hoods or dodgers can all increase the effect of the wind on the boat.

The tidal stream may increase or decrease the speed of the boat, or drift the whole boat in a turn. If there is a tidal stream present, always consider it as the most important factor in controlling the speed of the boat.

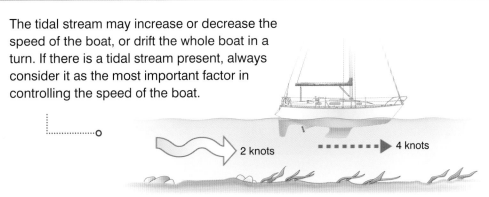

boat 4 knots + stream 2 knots = total 6 knots

The tidal stream can be used to slow the boat when coming up to a mooring or making a turn. When it is necessary to turn close to a buoy or beacon, the tidal stream can make a significant difference to the safe positioning of the boat.

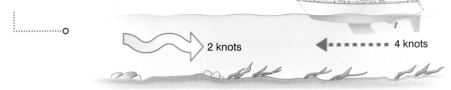

boat 4 knots - stream 2 knots = total 2 knots

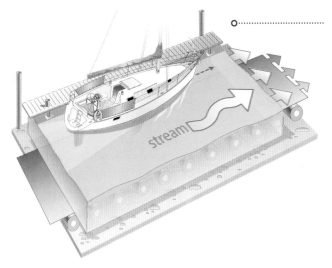

In a marina, the effect of the tidal stream can be seen by the pull on the mooring lines or the drift on weed and bubbles.

All this theory comes together for everyday manoeuvres such as making tight turns, coming alongside, berthing in marinas, anchoring and mooring.

Making a Simple Tight Turn

1. Put the rudder hard over and give a burst of power ahead. Return to neutral (A).

2. Watch the bow. It must keep moving sideways.

3. Give a burst of power in astern and let the propwalk pull the stern round (B). Do not reverse the rudder.

4. Give another burst of power ahead, if necessary (C).

5. Keep watching the bow to assess the turn.

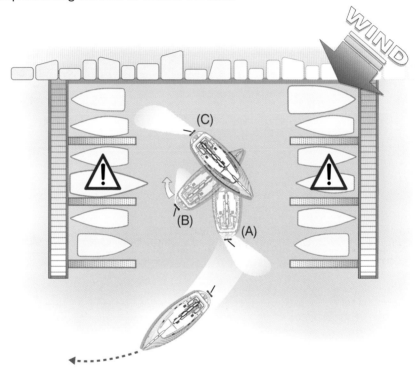

Remember that the aim is to turn, as near as possible, within the length of the boat. Monitor the progress of the turn by watching the sideways movement of the bow against the background. Do not let this stop. If it slows, use a burst of power ahead and then return to neutral. Remember the pivot point will be near the mast and consider the shape of the stern. The best way to turn will generally be dictated by which way the propwalk will pull the stern (it's therefore the same every time), but don't forget the wind or tidal stream.

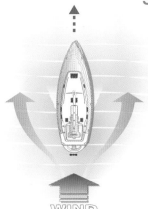

A serious amount of wind is likely to be obvious
and could be present in any marina. If this is the case,
make the initial turn into the wind. This will stop the
boat moving forwards and help to blow the bow round
once it is through the wind to bring the boat out of the
turn. If this is against the propwalk, don't use reverse at all
or it will stop the bow moving sideways. Let the wind do the work instead.
Turning downwind is best avoided. It will make the turning circle bigger as the boat
is blown forward and more power will be required to bring the bow into the wind.
More power and speed will make the turning circle bigger.

Tidal stream is a factor in some unenclosed marinas
and it may be less obvious than a stiff breeze. In this
case, always make the turn into the tidal stream to
avoid the increase of speed and the drift of the boat.

When positioning a boat within the turning space,
consider how the boat will drift with wind or tidal
stream. The middle may not be the best place to start;
it may be better to be a little upwind or uptide instead,
to allow for drift or leeway.

With so many factors to consider on top of the characteristics of the boat, practice
is the key to success, as well as plenty of strategically placed fenders and warps.
Brief the crew before all manoeuvres so they are not taken off-balance and know
what to do. Everyone needs to keep a good lookout for other boats moving.

How to Stop when there is no Brake

Using reverse too powerfully or for too long when coming to a berth or mooring
will slow the boat, but the propwalk will kick the stern sideways as well. Using
short bursts of astern will help to avoid this.

Reverse has a less powerful effect than forward. If the boat is moving forward fast
driven by wind or tidal stream from astern, using reverse will slow the boat but it
certainly won't stop it.

Coming Alongside

Arriving and Mooring at a Marina

Plan ahead and thoroughly prepare the boat before heading into the confined space of the marina. The crew should not be moving about in the helmsman's line of vision or hurriedly moving warps and fenders at the last minute.

How to do it:

1. Call the marina on the appropriate VHF channel for a berth, usually channel 80.
2. Put fenders on both sides of the boat; at least two where the beam is widest and one near the bow. A clove hitch is a good knot for fenders as the height can be changed quickly and the fender slid along the guardrail.
3. If there are plenty of crew, have someone ready with a roving fender.
4. Fenders for a pontoon need to be low, the base just clear of the water.
5. If coming alongside another boat, fenders need to be higher to protect the toerail.
6. You will need a minimum of six fenders of sufficient size, eight is better.

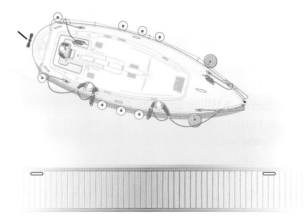

- Have mooring lines ready tied on both sides of the boat at the bow and the stern.
- Lead the end of the rope from outside the guardrail through the fairlead and secure it to the cleat. Do this even if you are coming into a berth which has permanent rigged lines – you may need warps to assist with stopping and the berth may be occupied by a visiting boat.

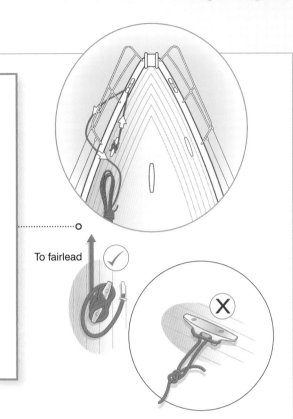

Make sure you have sufficient mooring warps – as a minimum you will need – four long and two shorter. Nylon three-strand or multi-plait is often used for anchor and mooring warps, as it is strong and has slight stretch. Additionally it does not float, which reduces the risk of it going round the propeller if it is dropped in the water. If a loop is required, tie a bowline. Do not have loops permanently made into the warps as they are likely to get snagged when used as a slip line.

To fairlead

- Brief the crew to stand amidships ready to step ashore. The crew nearest the bow can call distances if necessary.
- A stern line led aft, round a cleat, is the best way to slow the boat. Once the boat is stationary it is often easier to organise the lines from the side deck.
- Once ashore instruct crew to take a turn round a cleat and be ready to pull in or ease out. If the bow line is pulled too tight, the bow may swing in, making the stern swing out.

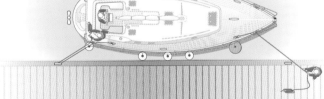

TIP Using coloured rope for fender lines is a great idea. One quick glance round the boat is enough to check that they are in the correct positions and are not left dangling over the side once out of the marina.

■ Remind everyone to keep a good lookout for other craft moving around the marina, especially motor cruisers, and not to block the helmsman's view! Lowering the sprayhood improves visibility.

■ Once the boat is in the correct position tie the bow and stern lines to keep the boat straight and springs to prevent surging.

■ If windy, remember the boat is not berthed safely until all the lines are in place.

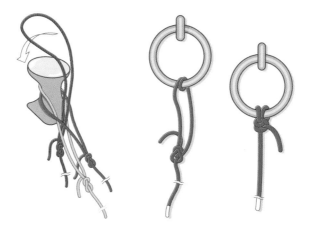

■ Use a separate line for each task; take the slack back onboard, each to a different cleat so they can be adjusted independently.

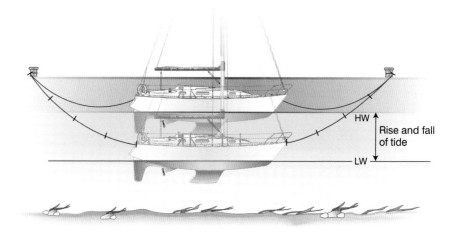

HW
Rise and fall of tide
LW

■ Mooring alongside a wall – check that there will be sufficient depth at low water and that the warps are long enough to allow for the fall – three or more times the maximum range will be required. To protect the boat use a fender board or fenders tied horizontally with a rope at each end.

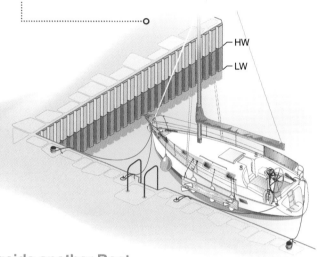

Rafting alongside another Boat

1. Ask permission (if they are aboard!) and when they will be leaving.

2. Tie up to the other boat.

3. Raise the fenders to protect the toerail.

4. Moor parallel to the other boat taking care that the spreaders or mast do not clash.

5. Take a long bow and stern line ashore so that the weight of your boat is not taken by the other boat's lines.

6. Remember when walking across other boats; go around the bow and never through the cockpit.

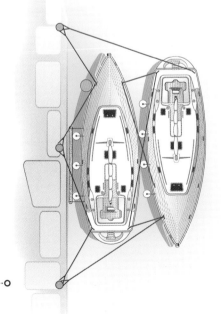

Coming Alongside

Berthing on a Finger Pontoon

The effect of wind and tidal stream on the speed and direction of the boat needs to be taken into consideration before coming alongside or mooring. Look for the signs of a strong tidal stream for example from weed or debris drifting past, if unsure, check the tide table for the direction. The effect often decreases in shallow water away from a deep channel. When berthing tidal stream is most likely to affect the speed of the boat and cause it to drift, so where possible always head into the tidal stream and keep uptide to allow for the drift.

Wind Effect

When the wind effect slows the speed of a boat, the bow has a tendency to blow downwind. Once in the marina the wind may decrease as buildings, walls or other boats provide shelter. Check the wind direction by looking at the movement of the water, flags in the marina and wind indicators on stationary boats.

- Wind from astern – consider lowering a sprayhood or it will act as a sail and push the boat forward.
- No wind or tide – approach at a shallow angle, aiming towards the front of the space and steering to bring the boat parallel to the pontoon. Control the speed by using slow ahead and neutral and then astern to stop.

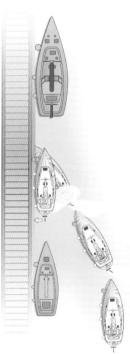

With an onshore or offshore wind the approach will be similar but the angle will be different.

1. Onshore wind – the risk is as it slows, first the bow and then the whole boat will blow towards the pontoon. To avoid this happening, aim at a much shallower angle, with the bow pointing slightly outwards. When using reverse, be aware of the effect of propwalk, it may pull the stern in and help keep the bow out, or do the opposite, increasing the risk of the bow being pushed towards the pontoon.

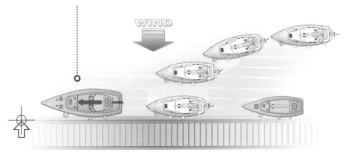

WIND

2. Offshore wind – aim for the middle of the space at a much sharper angle, do not turn away until close to the pontoon. Have the crew closer to the bow and ready to go ashore. Brief them to get a turn round a cleat quickly.

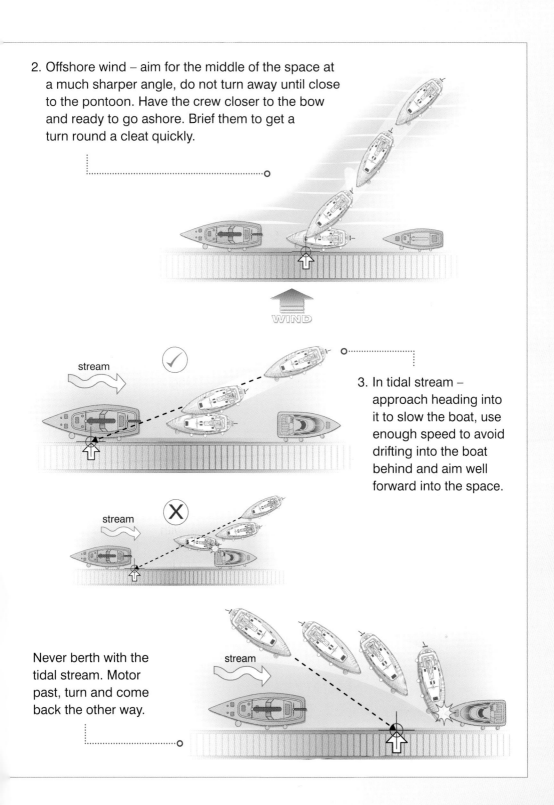

3. In tidal stream – approach heading into it to slow the boat, use enough speed to avoid drifting into the boat behind and aim well forward into the space.

Never berth with the tidal stream. Motor past, turn and come back the other way.

Coming Alongside

Ferry Gliding

If the alongside berth is very tight it may be possible to use the tidal stream to ferry glide the boat – a really useful skill to learn.

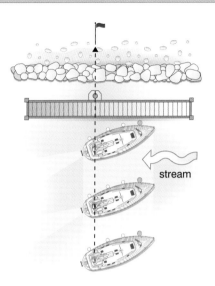

stream

1. Motor forward into the tidal stream at a speed to stem the tide – so the boat is holding its position relative to the pontoon.
2. Watch the background behind the pontoon and keep a transit (from a stationary fixture on land) to judge this. As there is water moving past the rudder the boat can be steered.
3. Angle the bow in slightly towards the pontoon and the tidal stream will drift the boat sideways. Never berth with the tidal stream behind you. Motor past, turn and come back the other way.

Berthing on a Finger Pontoon Shorter than the Boat

▮ The stern line cannot be used to slow the vessel and, if the stern line is pulled tight, it will move the boat forward.

▮ If the bow line is led aft as a brake, the stern may swing out if pulled too sharply. A midships cleat can be used instead. Rig a short line from this to a cleat on the pontoon, keep the engine in slow ahead with the rudder angled slightly inwards and the boat will maintain its position, this is especially useful if short handed.

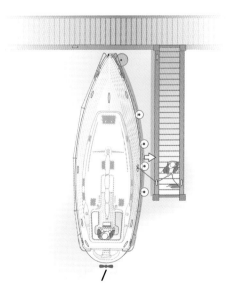

> **TIP** A good safety measure in the boat's permanent berth is to fix up a bow fender on the pontoon where the bow may touch.

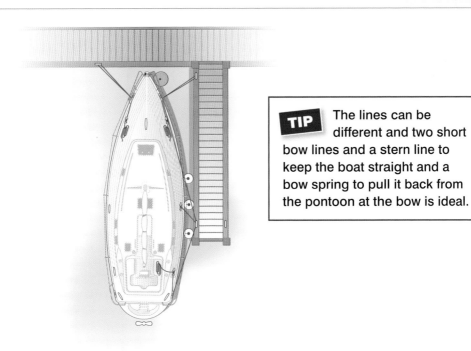

> **TIP** The lines can be different and two short bow lines and a stern line to keep the boat straight and a bow spring to pull it back from the pontoon at the bow is ideal.

Mooring in Locks

Coming into a lock is no different than coming alongside. However, conditions can be made difficult if the wind is funnelling through and there are tidal eddies near the entrance/exit. Space can be very limited and there may be lots of other boats manoeuvring.

Prepare the boat on both sides as usual and have a boathook ready in case an extended reach is necessary. Some big locks make life easy by having internal pontoons if not you may need to tie alongside another boat or to loop a rope through a vertical bar. Try not to use a fixed bollard if the boat is going to rise or fall. If there is no alternative, make sure the lines are long enough and so they can be used as slip lines, have no loops or knots.

It is important that the stern line goes on first and is eased out until the bow line is in place. Moor securely if the water moves through the lock quickly and monitor lines during the rise or fall.

Before slipping the lines to leave the lock remember the water flow inside the lock can be very powerful, so check the rudder is straight.

Using Rope Jammers

A jammer holds a rope securely, like a cleat.

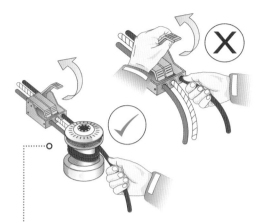

When releasing a rope under load, don't hold it close to the jammer. Take the strain on a winch.

Using Winches

Always wind the rope clockwise round the drum.

Add more turns for maximum friction.

When letting out, gently ease rope round drum with palm of hand.

Never wrap the rope around your hand.

Always have your thumbs uppermost – take care not to trap your fingers or thumbs between the rope and the winch.

Letting fly – flip the rope quickly off the drum to release rope when tacking or gybing.

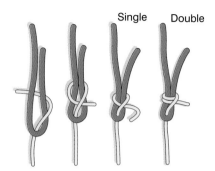

Single Double

Sheet bend

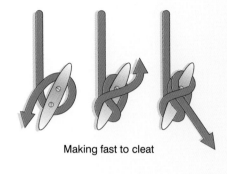

Making fast to cleat

Reef knot

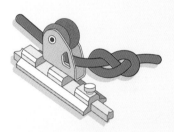

Figure of eight/Stop knot

Slides

Jams

Rolling hitch

Round turn and
two half hitches

Bowline

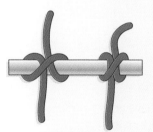

Clove hitch

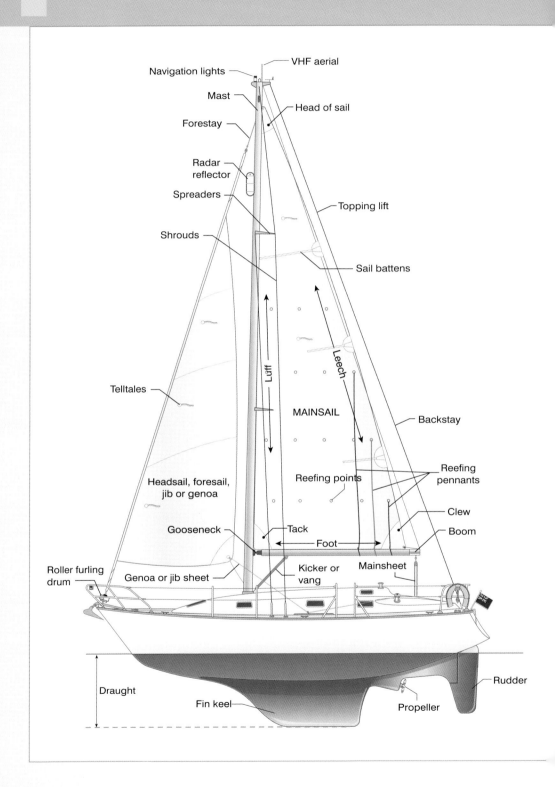

VHF aerial

Navigation lights

Mast

Head of sail

Forestay

Radar reflector

Spreaders

Topping lift

Shrouds

Sail battens

Luff

Leech

Telltales

MAINSAIL

Backstay

Headsail, foresail, jib or genoa

Reefing points

Reefing pennants

Gooseneck

Tack

Foot

Clew

Boom

Roller furling drum

Genoa or jib sheet

Kicker or vang

Mainsheet

Draught

Rudder

Fin keel

Propeller

Points of Sailing

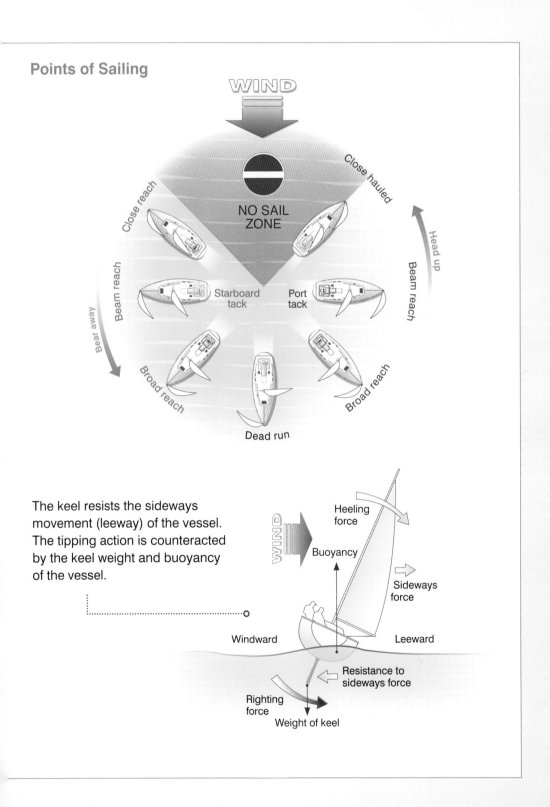

The keel resists the sideways movement (leeway) of the vessel. The tipping action is counteracted by the keel weight and buoyancy of the vessel.

Raising and Lowering Sails – The Skipper's Role

The skipper must at all times keep a watch on the general safety of the boat and crew. This is easier if the skipper is not too "hands on" with the task and has briefed the crew beforehand so they know what to do and when.

- Choose a sheltered area rather than the open sea
- Consider whether the crew need to be clipped on
- Keep clear of a busy channel
- Keep a good lookout all around for other boats and water users
- Monitor the depth, or use the echo sounder alarm

Understanding the routines for raising, lowering and reefing sails makes it easier to organise the boat and crew efficiently. Prepare both sails before leaving the shore, and remember to check:

- Mainsheet coils have been undone and the cover removed or unzipped
- Main halyard has been attached correctly and secured so the sail does not start lifting
- In the case of a hanked-on jib, have the sheets in place and the sail secured to the top guard rail.

Before raising the sails:

1. Check the main hatch is closed when crew are working on the coach roof
2. Don't let crew stand between the mast and mainsheet once the sail begins to go up and the boom is free to swing
3. Ensure that when halyards and sheets are under load, the weight is always taken on a winch and ropes are never wrapped around anyone's hand.

Why is it a good idea to put the main up first? Although not essential there are many advantages in doing so.

1. The direction the boat must point is critical while raising the main because the sail must be flapping as it goes up.
2. If the genoa is flogging at the same time, the sail and the sheets will be a hazard to crew standing in front of the mast.
3. The noise level will make it hard to communicate.
4. The view for the helmsman will be even more restricted.

Raising the Main

1. Release the sail ties.

2. Head the boat with the wind about 30° off the bow so that the sail flaps as it is being raised. Choose the side which allows the boom to swing away from the crew as they winch the halyard, if possible.

3. Position the crew in front of the boom (or in the cockpit) clear of the boom and then release the mainsheet and kicking strap(vang).

4. Raise the sail through an open jammer, watching that the sail or halyard does not get caught on the rigging.

5. Close the jammer and winch it tight, checking the luff of the sail. Too much tension will produce vertical creases – too little and the luff will be baggy.

6. Pull in the mainsheet and ease the topping lift.

7 Tighten the kicking strap, check the clew outhaul and stow the halyard.

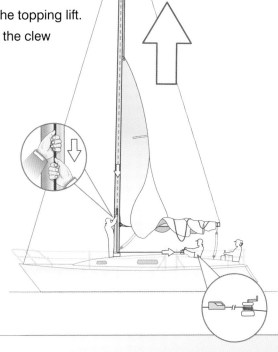

The tension may need adjusting if the wind strength changes. With a stronger wind it may be necessary to tighten the halyard or clew outhaul.

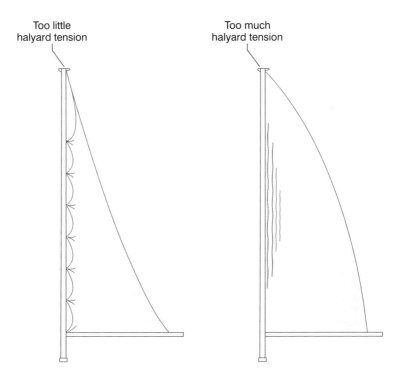

Too little
halyard tension

Too much
halyard tension

Hoisting the jib is very simple, especially if it is a roller-furling sail.

- Pull on the sheet on the leeward side while easing out on the furling line.
- Have the sheet on a winch and the furling line with a turn on a cleat to keep the sail under control.
- Many furling sails are very large genoas and it is not necessary to unfurl them completely.
- Less sail will give better control on a windy day and the helmsman a better view. Remember to move the genoa car forward with a smaller sail to put equal tension on the leech and the foot of the sail.

Lowering and Bagging the Sails

Before lowering sails, choose a suitable area, clear of other boats and allow plenty of time. Remember to check that there are no lines in the water before starting the engine.

Normally lowering or furling the jib first makes everything easier. As with raising sails, being without the jib when dealing with the main gives a better view for the helmsman and removes the risk of being hit by a flying jib sheet. Unlike the mainsail, it can be done without heading the boat into the wind.

With a furling jib just pull in on the furling line while keeping a little tension on the sheet to be sure that the sail is neatly furled.

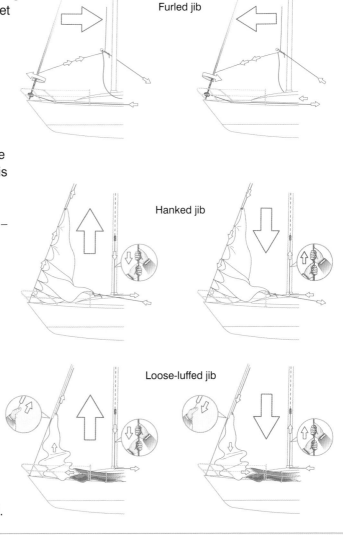

Furled jib

Hanked jib

Loose-luffed jib

Once the sail is pulled in there will be a long length of furling line in the cockpit. Coil and stow this to prevent the possibility of it going over the side and fouling the propeller – an expensive mistake!

If the jib is to be lowered

■ Keep some tension on the sheet as the halyard is slackened to prevent the sail going in the water.

■ Once the sail is down, clip the halyard on to the pulpit and pull it tight.

■ Pull the sail aft and tie it against the guardrail.

Lowering and Bagging the Main

1. Station one crew member by the mast ready to pull down on the luff of the sail when the halyard is released.

2. Let the kicking strap (vang) and mainsheet go, pull up on the topping lift to take the weight of the boom and raise it slightly – this will encourage the sail to flap.

3. Head up, close enough to the wind to ensure that the sail flaps as the halyard is released and the sail is pulled down.

4. Secure the halyard, pull the mainsheet tight and ensure that the main hatch is pulled across before the crew go on deck to bag the sail.

5. Push all the sail to the leeward side of the boom and make a bag on the other side. Pull the sail along backwards in big folds and push them into the bag.

6. Once all the sail and loose reefing pennants are in the bag, roll it tight and secure it to the boom with sail ties.

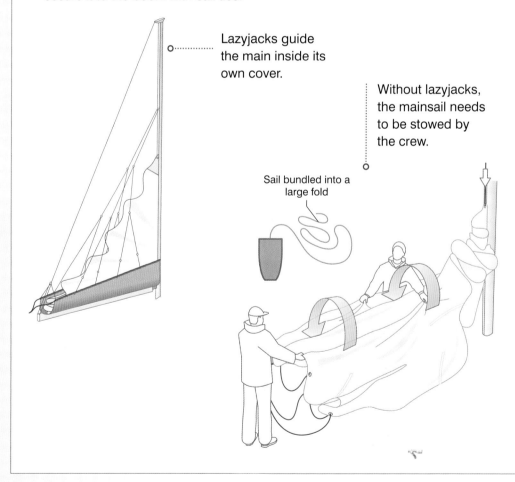

Lazyjacks guide the main inside its own cover.

Without lazyjacks, the mainsail needs to be stowed by the crew.

Sail bundled into a large fold

Alternatively, the mainsail can be flaked (folded across the boom and secured).

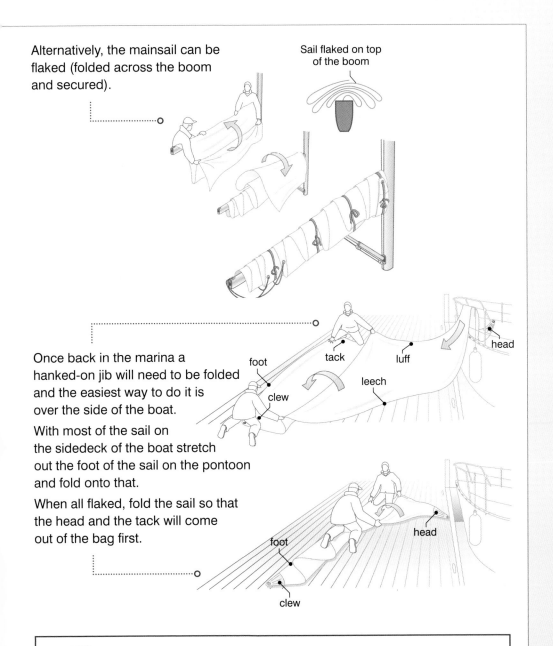

Sail flaked on top of the boom

Once back in the marina a hanked-on jib will need to be folded and the easiest way to do it is over the side of the boat.

With most of the sail on the sidedeck of the boat stretch out the foot of the sail on the pontoon and fold onto that.

When all flaked, fold the sail so that the head and the tack will come out of the bag first.

foot   tack   luff   head

clew   leech

foot   head

clew

TIP When sails are being raised and lowered, watch for signs of wear on the halyards and sheets. These ropes are usually made from polyester because of its low stretch and strength, and braid-on-braid construction because it is more comfortable to handle. Washing them at the end of the season will help them remain in good condition.

Boat Handling under Sail

How the Boat Turns and Steers under Sail

The best way to find out how the sails really work and the boat steers and turns is to try a few manoeuvres. Choose a reasonable day and a good clear space when there are not too many other boats about. Use the full main and a no. 1 size jib.

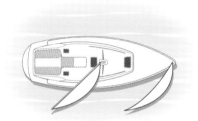

Put the boat onto a beam reach with the wind on the side of the boat. The waves are a good guide to the wind direction.

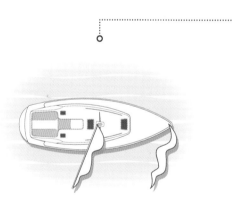

Let the sheets go completely so the sails flap out sideways from the boat like flags. On some boats, depending on the rig, the wind may need to be slightly forward of the beam for this to happen. This is likely with a fractionally rigged boat where the forestay does not go to the top of the mast and the spreaders are raked back. The noise of the flogging sails may be annoying but it is not dangerous for a crew in the cockpit and clear of the sheets.

The boat will lose speed and eventually stop; how quickly depends on several things, such as the shape and weight of the boat, and how windy it is. Strangely, the boat will stop more quickly on a windy day as the sails flap more vigorously.

The log will show this loss of speed through the water, but the boat may move over the ground due to the tidal stream or current. As the speed is lost, the effect of the wind on the hull may be felt too.

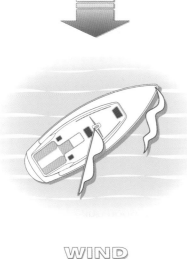

Head up into the wind on to a close reach, so the wind is forward of the beam, before all steerage way is lost. Both sails will continue to flap – indeed the main may flap more.

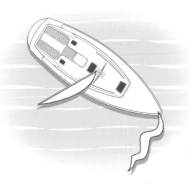

Now bear away from the wind on to a broad reach with the wind aft of the beam, on the quarter of the boat. The mainsail will stop flapping and the boat will begin to pick up speed again. Exactly when this happens will again depend on the rig. The mainsail starts working again when the boom rests on the shrouds. The jib does not have the same problem, so continues to flap.

When it comes to anchoring, picking up moorings and any other manoeuvre under sail, when you need to slow down or stop this means that because the mainsail will not always flap, it may be necessary to take it down in advance. Even then the boat may drift with the tidal stream or make leeway from the wind.

The boat will not stop unless both sails are flapping, or have been taken down.

The main will not flap if the wind is from aft of the beam.

This is also why when the boat 'goes about' from one tack to the other, turning the bow through the wind, both the sails flap and speed is lost until the sails are sheeted in again on the other side.

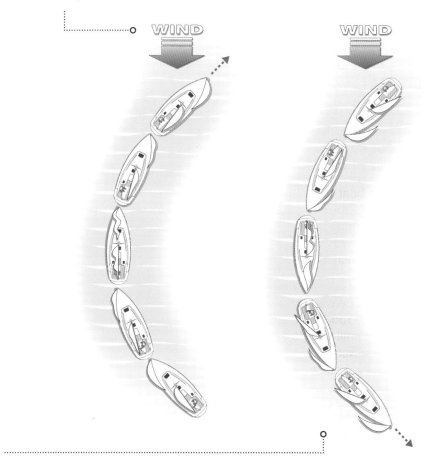

When the boat gybes from one tack to another this does not happen. In a gybe, the boat is turned so that the stern goes through the wind; the main does not flap but crosses powerfully from one side to the other. If the gybe is not controlled, by pulling in the boom before moving the rudder, the boom can move across the boat dangerously fast from the power of the wind and from the distance of the swing. Pulling in the main uses the strength of the mainsheet and its blocks to take the weight. It is necessary to do this every time, not just on a windy day. The bad habit of pulling the mainsheet across or catching it as it passes can lead to injury. Once the boom has come across it needs to be eased out quickly and carefully too, to help the helmsman straighten up. Boat speed is not lost in a gybe because the sails are working most of the time.

How do the Sails Work?

Again, the best way to find this out is by experimentation. Put the boat on to a beam reach, or a little closer to the wind if necessary, so that both the main and the jib are flapping. Hold the tiller or the wheel so that the rudder is straight and allow the boat to slow down and stop. Sheet in just the jib, enough for it to start working, while continuing to keep the rudder straight. Watch the bow against the background to see what happens.

Under jib alone the boat will bear away. This is because the bow of the boat has a natural tendency to blow away from the wind, pivoting on the keel, and the jib has increased this.

Try the same with the main. Start with the boat beam on to the wind, both sails flapping and the rudder straight. Pull in just the main until it starts driving the boat and watch the bow. Under main alone the boat will head up towards the wind. The sails work together to give the boat a tendency to go straight if the sails are balanced, both in size and sheeting tension.

When the boat alters course the sheets will need to be adjusted. If this does not happen, when the boat heads up closer to the wind the sails will flap, unless they were too tight beforehand. When bearing away don't forget to ease out the sheets. There will be no flapping of the sails as a reminder. Forgetting to adjust sheets will cause a loss of performance and the tendency of the boat to go straight may be affected.

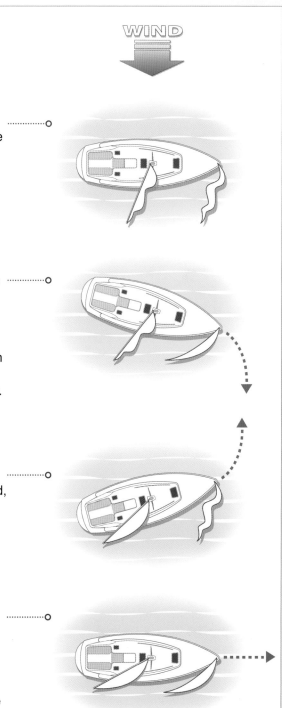

To judge the adjustment an excellent guide is the telltales on the luff of the headsail. These show the flow of air over the sail. On a close reach, the telltales on both sides of the sail should stream out horizontally. If the one on the windward side starts to flap, the boat is heading too close to the wind and should bear away. If the one on the back of the sail flaps, then head up closer to the wind.

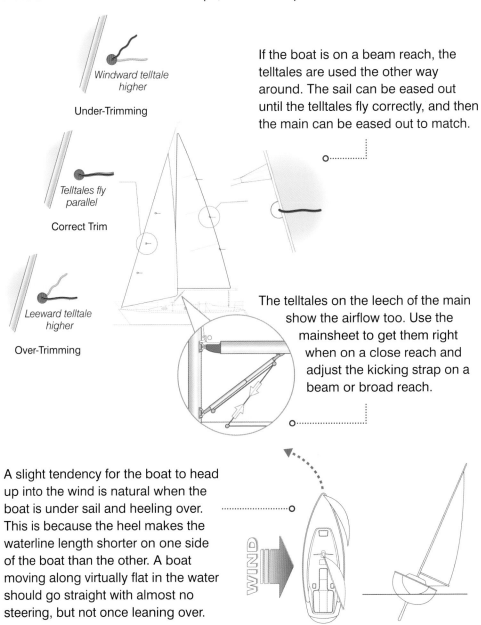

Windward telltale
higher

Under-Trimming

Telltales fly
parallel

Correct Trim

Leeward telltale
higher

Over-Trimming

If the boat is on a beam reach, the telltales are used the other way around. The sail can be eased out until the telltales fly correctly, and then the main can be eased out to match.

The telltales on the leech of the main show the airflow too. Use the mainsheet to get them right when on a close reach and adjust the kicking strap on a beam or broad reach.

A slight tendency for the boat to head up into the wind is natural when the boat is under sail and heeling over. This is because the heel makes the waterline length shorter on one side of the boat than the other. A boat moving along virtually flat in the water should go straight with almost no steering, but not once leaning over.

WIND

If this slight tendency increases enough to make the steering heavy or hard work just to go straight, then the boat is out of balance. Using the knowledge of how each sail affects the steering of the boat, it should be possible to work out which sail is working too hard, because it is too big or sheeted too tight.

The most common problem is weather helm, when the boat has a consistent tendency to head up, making it hard to control, especially in a gust. As the boat heads up, it heels more, which makes the problem worse. In this case it is the main that is the problem. Ease the mainsheet in the gust to regain control, and then reef the main to avoid it happening again. Some people are reluctant to reef, thinking that reducing the size of the mainsail will slow the boat, but the opposite is true. Reefing will decrease the weather helm, allowing the helmsman to keep the rudder straighter, reducing the drag. Boats often gain speed by reefing. Also, the boat will be flatter in the water, and the tendency to head up will be less. Life on the boat will be more convenient too for anyone navigating, cooking, sleeping or in the heads.

The opposite of weather helm is lee helm, when the boat has a tendency to bear away. In this case it is the jib that is working too hard or is too big in relation to the main.

Generally, sail the boat as flat as possible. If the boat suddenly heels over and heads up into the wind, 'dump' the main by letting the mainsheet out quickly to lose speed and regain control. Then reef to stop it happening again.

Remember how the sails work and feel how the boat is going, which will be affected by the sea conditions as well as the wind strength. The boat's heading in relation to the wind will make a difference too. At sea, the wave pattern may be very different from that in a river with the same wind force. Listen to the forecast before every trip, get updates at every opportunity and don't be fooled in a sheltered berth or river.

The best way to feel how the boat is going is by taking the wheel or the tiller and considering:

- Is the steering heavy with a tendency to head up? Check the main. It may be too big or too tight.
- If you start to think about reefing, do it. It can easily come out again if necessary.
- Is the boat bearing away consistently? It is the jib this time that is working too hard, so check the sheet tension or make the sail smaller.
- Is the boat losing speed, not pushing through the waves but bouncing along? The wind may have eased. Sea conditions take longer to moderate so less wind goes unnoticed. It may be time to take the reef out.

Reefing the Sails

Too much sail on a windy day makes a boat uncomfortable and difficult to steer. Heavy steering, excessive heel and a tendency to broach in gusts are signs that you need to reef the boat.

WIND

NO SAIL ZONE

When the main is to be reefed, a crew member will have to go forward of the mast and clipping on is recommended. The process is exactly the same as for lowering the sail, except that the sail will only come down sufficiently for the cringle to be hooked onto the ram's horn.

- Steer the boat close enough to the wind so that the main flaps when the mainsheet is released.
- This will take the power out of the sail, making putting in the reef easier and preventing damage to the sail.
- The jib can still be sheeted in to give the helmsman steerage way and avoid the sail and jibsheet flapping dangerously near the crew at the mast.
- Put the boat on whichever tack will make the boom and mainsheet swing away from the crew working on the halyard and pennants in the cockpit.

> **TIP** There will be considerable weight on both the furling line and the sheet, so keep turns around the winch or on a cleat and remember that ropes should never be wrapped around the hand.

When putting in a reef, always do the halyard first and then the pennant. When taking out the reef, reverse the order, releasing the reef knots and pennant first.

Putting in a reef or taking one out safely and quickly is important and well worth practising in good weather to avoid a struggle in bad conditions. If there is any doubt about controlling the boat or there being a lack of room for the manoeuvre put the engine on to assist the helmsman.

1. Prepare by easing out the kicking strap and mainsheet.
2. Pull up on the topping lift to take the weight of the boom and head close enough to the wind so the main flaps, just as for lowering the sail.
3. Ease the halyard and hook the cringle (ring) onto the ram's horn, then tighten the halyard again.
4. When the pennant is tight, ease the topping lift and pull in the mainsheet and kicking strap.
5. Tie the sail to the boom using a reef knot and tidy all the other lines.

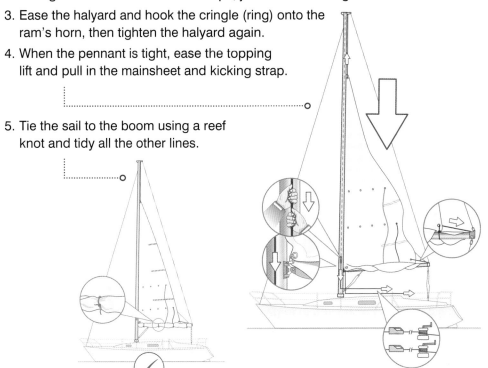

One of the many advantages of a furling jib is the ease with which it can be adjusted to suit the conditions. When reducing the size of the sail it is important to keep the size in balance with the main and not forget to move the genoa cars forward to maintain the correct sheeting angle.

Without a furling sail, the genoa will need to come down and be replaced with a smaller jib. The hanks of the new sail can be attached to the forestay and the lazy jibsheet tied on before the genoa is lowered.

no 1 genoa

no 2 genoa

no 1 jib or working jib

storm jib

Heaving To

Heave To sounds like something out of a Hornblower novel, when a ship could lie stopped in the water and surprisingly most modern yachts can do this too. It will take practice to find out how your boat will lie and in reality stopped is a relative term. The boat may forereach a little, will definitely make leeway and be drifting on the tidal stream. So, before Heaving To, check that the position is safe and that there are not too many other craft close by always remembering that the COLREGS still apply.

The easiest way to Heave To:

- Go about but without releasing the jibsheet.
- The jib will then back and push the bow away from the wind, while the main tries to make the boat head up.
- It should be possible to steer into the wind but may require you to adjust the sheets to keep the boat as static as possible.
- Although the boat may not stop and will drift and make leeway, it will be settled and steady – useful to get onboard jobs done on a rough day.

Sailing Downwind

Sailing downwind can be deceptively peaceful and relaxing. When the wind is from abaft the beam, its strength can be underestimated and any increase may go unnoticed. When sunny and calm it is easy to forget that, in an accidental gybe, the strength of the wind and the weight of the boom can cause serious injury to crew knocked off balance or hit by the boom or mainsheet.

It is potentially dangerous to sail with the wind directly behind the boat.

- A gybe can occur – due to a slight alteration in course or wind shift.
- On a broad reach – watch for the ominous sign of the jib collapsing if the helmsman bears away too much due to the wind shadow of the main.
- If the boat is running dead downwind it can goose wing – jib one side and main the other.
- When cruising downwind a preventer should be rigged. Even on a broad reach a preventer is a good idea to stop the boom coming across suddenly in an accidental gybe.

Explain to the crew:

■ The warning sign from the jib of an imminent gybe and the need to head up a little if this happens

■ Places to avoid sitting or standing when the boat is sailing downwind – these differ from boat to boat. It may be better to sit towards the back of the cockpit away from the mainsheet traveller near the companionway, or the reverse

■ The mainsheet and its associated blocks can be as dangerous as the boom in an accidental gybe

■ No sitting, standing or sunbathing on the coach roof.

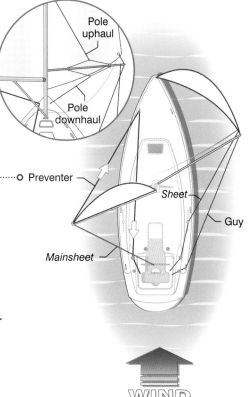

Pole uphaul

Pole downhaul

Preventer

Sheet

Guy

Mainsheet

WIND

Rigging a Preventer

A preventer must be rigged safely.

■ Attach one end of the rope to the end of the boom. Do not lean over the side of the boat to do this. Alter course and pull the boom in towards the boat with the mainsheet.

■ The rope should be long enough to lead from the end of the boom to the foredeck and back to the cockpit making it quick to release if required.

■ Although easier to set up, a preventer should not be fixed to the boom at the kicking strap attachment point and led to the toerail.

Mediterranean Mooring

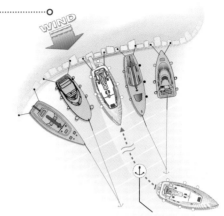

Extensively in the Mediterranean, boats are moored either bows to or stern to a quay. Stern to has the advantage of making it easier to get on and off the boat, not so private for anyone sitting or eating in the cockpit!

1. Prepare two shore lines from the bow or stern and put fenders on both sides of the boat.

2. Drop the anchor about four boat lengths out from the quay and motor into position.

Anchor four boat lengths from quay

Some harbour authorities have installed lazy lines attached to the quay and the seabed to avoid the need to drop the anchor. They are picked up by crew when on the quay or with the boathook if there is a pickup buoy.

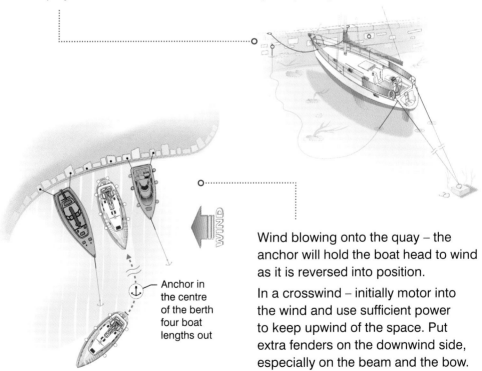

Anchor in the centre of the berth four boat lengths out

Wind blowing onto the quay – the anchor will hold the boat head to wind as it is reversed into position.

In a crosswind – initially motor into the wind and use sufficient power to keep upwind of the space. Put extra fenders on the downwind side, especially on the beam and the bow.

Leaving a Pontoon, Marina or Raft

Before releasing any lines, assess the situation and decide on how the manoeuvre should be done, prepare the boat and brief the crew.

- Make sure that the boat is ready to leave, everything is stowed and the electricity line to the shore has been disconnected.

- Check the wind and tidal stream taking into account the effect they will have on the boat. Is the boat being pushed forward in the berth or will the bow blow off as soon as the line is slackened?

- Remember the pivot point of the boat, if the boat is turned away from a pontoon or another boat at too sharp an angle the other end may swing in and touch.

- Position extra fenders. If motoring out ahead, put a fender on the quarter, reversing, put a fender near the bow to allow for the pivoting effect.

- Take off as many mooring lines as possible and make the others into slip lines, so they lead back onto the boat with a short end to let go. Do not have a long length of rope or one with a loop as it may get snagged as the boat moves away.

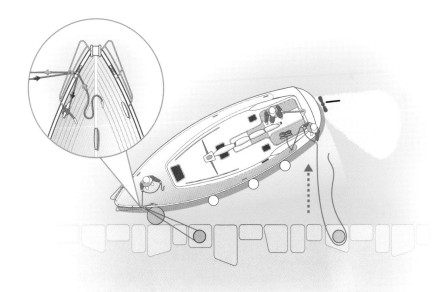

■ It is impossible to make a rule as to which mooring lines should come off first. It depends on the circumstances, the wind and the tidal stream.
If in doubt, ease each line and see what happens.
If the boat surges forward or veers off then re-tighten the rope and think again.

■ Try to anticipate what effect the propwalk will have when the boat starts reversing.

■ Check all around for other boats that are moving before letting go.

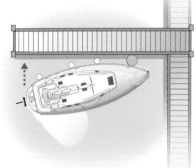

An offshore wind may help by blowing the bow and then the boat off the pontoon. Remove the springs and put a fender on the quarter. Make the bow and stern lines into slip lines.

If the wind is strong, rig the new slip lines before removing the original ones. When ready to leave, slip the bow line, let the bow blow off then slip the stern line.

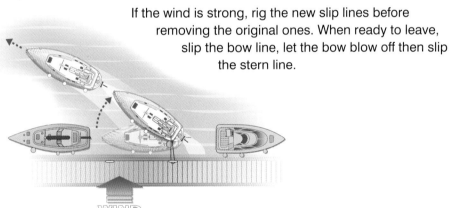

WIND

In an onshore wind it will not be so easy to motor away so springing off may help. This uses the shape of the boat and the power of the engine against a spring to change the boat's angle and has the advantage of being easier if there are fewer crew members on the boat because, once everything is prepared, all the lines can be removed except for the spring being used. It is important that the spring comes off at just the right moment so have crew ready with a short piece of rope without loops or knots ready to slip. Brief the crew on what you are doing and what they must do and when ready make the instruction to let go very clear and ask them to confirm.

Stern Spring – allows the boat to spring off very effectively if the wind is just off the bow, but not if it is on the beam.

Put a fender on the quarter, remove the stern line and reverse against a stern spring, the bow will come out up to about 30° or 40°, depending on the shape of the boat.

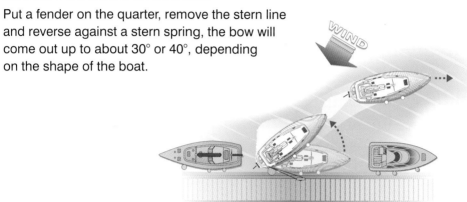

This may not be enough to clear the boat ahead (especially if the bow has not come out close to or through the wind) because as soon as the boat stops reversing the bow will start to blow back in. If this happens, simply stop reversing and the boat will blow back into its original position.

In a Beam Wind – use a bow spring and forward power. Put a fender near the bow, remove the stern line and go ahead against a bow spring. The stern will come out. The angle will be much greater this time because of the shape of the bow. The boat can then reverse out.

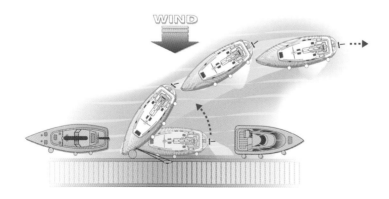

Springing off can also be used in a
marina berth if the propwalk or wind
will cause the stern to come too
close to the pontoon.

In some very tight situations one solution
is to turn the boat under warps to point the other
way. Remove the springs and rig ropes and fenders on the offside ready for the
turn. Lead them round either the bow or the stern. Turn the boat the way that it
wants to go, bow away from the wind, and the wind will then help.

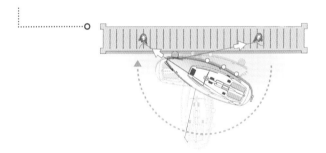

Warps can also be used to pull the bow out if there is not enough room to use the
engine. Extra fenders and long lines will be needed and it is essential that they do
not snag, so lead them carefully and avoid knots and loops.

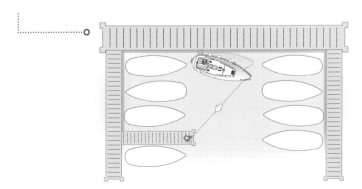

If there is tidal stream from astern, use a bow spring and then motor out astern or the tidal stream may drift the boat forward into the yacht in front.

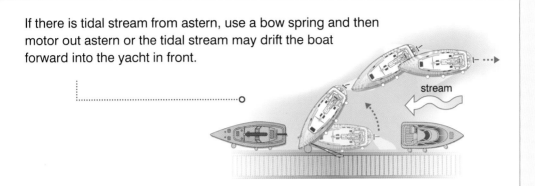

If the tidal stream is from ahead, using a stern spring will bring the bow out into the tidal stream and the boat can motor away.

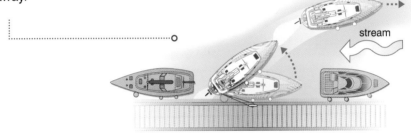

Leaving from a raft when inside of another boat is another situation requiring care. As with turning the boat under warps, preparation is very important. The outside boat must have shorelines for both bow and stern in place and led correctly so that the boat can be pulled in as the gap opens.

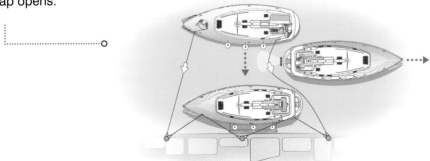

Picking up a Mooring Buoy

Having selected a mooring in a sheltered position, look to see what there is to pick up. There could be a pick-up buoy supporting the mooring loop, just a rope loop, or a metal ring.

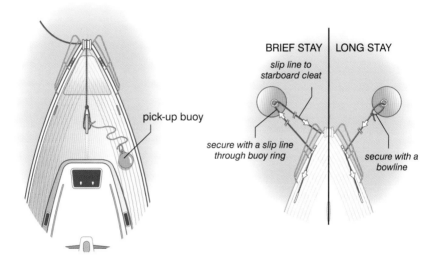

pick-up buoy

BRIEF STAY | LONG STAY

slip line to starboard cleat

secure with a slip line through buoy ring

secure with a bowline

Choose a mooring where the other boats in the trot are of similar size, or larger, as a guide that the mooring is strong enough for the boat. Check that there will be sufficient depth at low water.

To calculate what the clearance will be at low water, check the depth with the echo sounder and from this subtract:

- ■ The draught of the boat
- ■ The fall of the tide (the height of tide at the time of picking up the mooring minus low water height)

See page 83 for how to calculate the height of tide.

Have two crew members on the foredeck, if possible, with the boathook and a mooring line ready. They can point towards the buoy and call the distances back to the helmsman, who will probably not be able to see the buoy once close.

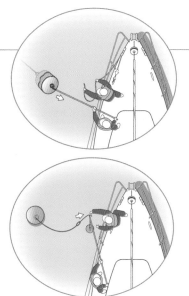

The crew must be prepared to lean down towards the buoy to get the pick-up line or to loop through a rope. The mooring may be very heavy so it should be secured quickly by leading the mooring loop or the boat's own mooring line through a fairlead or over the bow roller to a cleat. If the mooring loop goes on to a cleat it should be secured with another rope over the top. When mooring to a metal ring, only use a slip line for a short stop, because of chafe. For an overnight stay use a round turn and a bowline and a separate, slacker line for added security.

Which way to Approach the Buoy

Under power this is almost instinctive from looking at the other boats on the trot.

Once moored, the boat will lie in the same direction as all the similar boats close by. The approach should be made as close to that heading as possible.

The direction will be affected by:

- Tidal stream, almost always the most important consideration
- Wind direction

The shape of the boat will make a difference too. The tidal stream will have far less influence on a motor boat with no keel than a yacht. For a yacht, the tidal stream is so important that it will usually determine the direction the boat lies even if there is a strong wind. Sometimes a yacht will be pushed forward over the mooring buoy by a wind over the stern. A sprayhood and dodgers will only

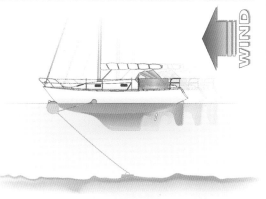

make this worse. It can be quite difficult to stop the boat and pick up a mooring under these conditions, and possibly uncomfortable once moored.

Once the decision has been made, brief the crew and give them time to get prepared. Ensure that the approach speed is controlled. Monitor it with a transit on the beam to assess the progress against the tidal stream. Always aim to put the mooring on the windward bow. This is safest because if there is a problem and the crew are not able to pick up the mooring, the bow's natural tendency to blow downwind will make it easier to manoeuvre away from the buoy, come round and have another go. The most important thing is not to run over the buoy.

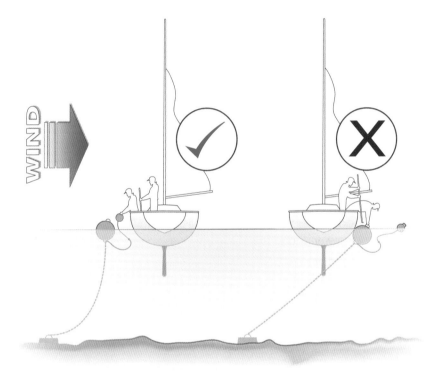

Mooring under Sail

Exactly the same rules apply if approaching under sail. Head into the tidal stream as close as possible to the way that the boat will lie once it is moored. The choice of which sail or sails to use comes from the wind angle on this heading.

Look at similar boats nearby or sail past the mooring to test the conditions and check the depth.

Consider space if mooring under sail. Make sure there is room to approach the mooring, and the depth and space to sail past if the boat is too fast to do the pick up or loses too much speed to be able to reach it. Remember that once all speed has been lost a yacht will take time to pick it up again, which requires space. Try not to let the boat go head to wind with the sails flapping or it will drift with the tidal stream and make leeway uncontrollably.

In rivers the wind conditions can vary within quite a short distance because of trees or gusts down small valleys. Monitor the speed using a transit on the beam and never try for a pickup if the boat is going too fast.

Which Sail or Sails to use

This is dictated by the basic theory of how the sails work and the direction that the boat will lie once it is on the mooring. Imagine a boat already on the mooring and about to sail off. Which sail or sails would it be possible to raise?

This depends on the wind direction on the mooring and which sail would flap as it was being raised. The jib will always flap of course, but the main will only flap if the wind is from forward of the beam.

Picking up a Mooring

If the wind is from aft of the beam the main will not flap on the approach, even if the sheet is released fully, so the boat will not be able to stop.

Sail upwind to gain space, then drop the main and pick up the mooring on a broad reach or a run. Part furl the jib to give a better view, reduce the speed and make it easier and safer for the crew on the foredeck.
Monitor the speed using a transit on the beam.

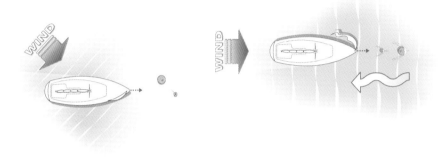

If the wind is from forward of the beam, both sails will flap on the approach when the sheets are released. The main can be used, and the jib too if necessary.

Approach the mooring on a reach between a beam reach and a close reach using just the main if there is sufficient speed. Let the main out to check that it will flap and then control the speed by grabbing the mainsheet to "fill and spill". Watch for the boat making leeway by using a transit with the mooring ahead.

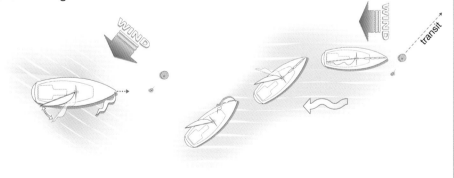

To "fill and spill", let the main right out on the mainsheet so that it flaps to slow the boat. Grab the whole of the mainsheet to gain a little extra way. Another way to reduce speed is to release the kicking strap and mainsheet and then push up on the boom or pull the topping lift up quite high. This is called scandalising the main.

A strong bucket can be tied on and thrown over the side to increase drag.

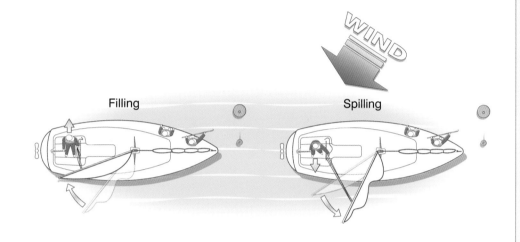

Anchoring

There are several different types of anchor that might be on the boat together with the chain and warp.

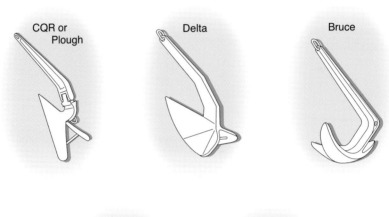

CQR or Plough

Delta

Bruce

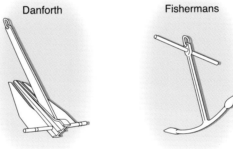

Danforth

Fishermans

Stowing

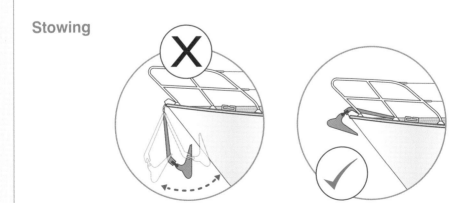

The amount of chain and warp used must be far more than the depth of water to allow a good length of chain to lie on the seabed. This provides a horizontal pull on the anchor and makes it dig in. If too little scope is let out the boat may drag its anchor at high water. Mark the chain and warp in some way so it is easy to prepare the correct amount.

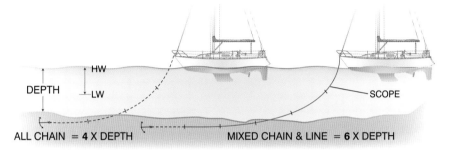

With chain, use four times the maximum depth and with a combination of chain and warp use six times. This means that it is important to allow plenty of room behind the boat when anchoring and for the swing, remembering that not all boats will turn at the same time. Yachts will lie with the tidal stream and motor boats more often to the wind.

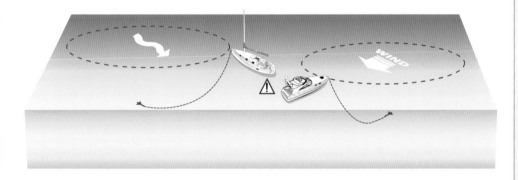

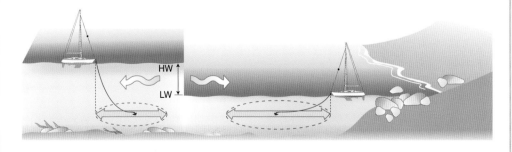

Anchoring

Choosing a Good Anchorage

Thing to consider:

- Shelter from the wind
- The weather forecast in case the wind changes direction
- The nature of the seabed shown on the chart. Mud and sand are better than rock or shingle
- Space behind the boat
- Whether there is enough room to swing when the tide turns
- Check on the chart for a recommended anchorage
- Look in the pilot book for advice or warnings
- The boat must be outside any channel used by other boats, including if it swings
- The depth of water. It may be necessary to work out the minimum depth of water in which to anchor to be sure that the boat will not ground at low water.

To calculate the minimum depth of water to anchor, add together:

- The draught of the boat
- The minimum clearance required at low water
- The fall of the tide (the height of the tide at the time of anchoring minus low water height)

See page 83 for how to calculate the height of tide.

Once the position has been selected, prepare the anchor and chain on the foredeck. Flake out the required amount of chain and secure it to the cleat. Do this carefully so that the first turn from the anchor, which is under load, comes to the base of the cleat with the securing turns on top. This is so that the length can be adjusted despite the weight of the anchor.

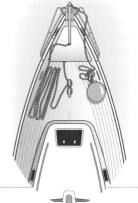

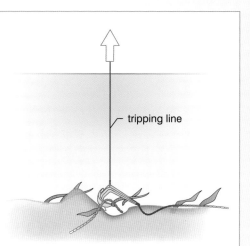

tripping line

In addition to the anchor and chain a trip line could be used in an area where there may be problems with fouling. This is a small buoy attached to the front of the anchor to help pull it in the opposite direction to free it. If using a trip line, make sure that the rope is long enough at high water and that it does not get caught up round the pulpit when the anchor is being laid.

If anchoring under power, motor in the direction that the boat will lie once anchored, usually into the tidal stream. Once the boat has stopped and begins to drift backwards, pay the chain out slowly. This will ensure that the chain is laid out on the seabed rather than in a heap. Let the boat settle and then check that the anchor is holding using a transit or a bearing on the beam. If the boat is dragging, let out more chain if there is room and then check again.

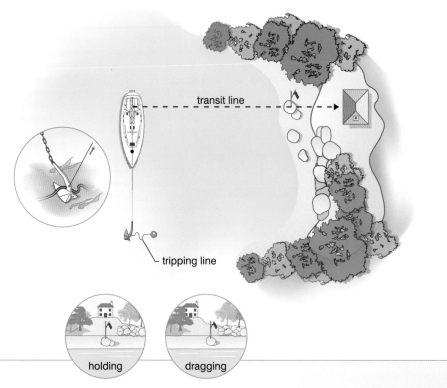

transit line

tripping line

holding   dragging

If anchoring under sail, the principles of which way to approach and which sail to use are exactly the same as with picking up a mooring. Anchoring under sail is easier because the boat has to be stopped before the anchor is paid out but, usually, the position is less critical.

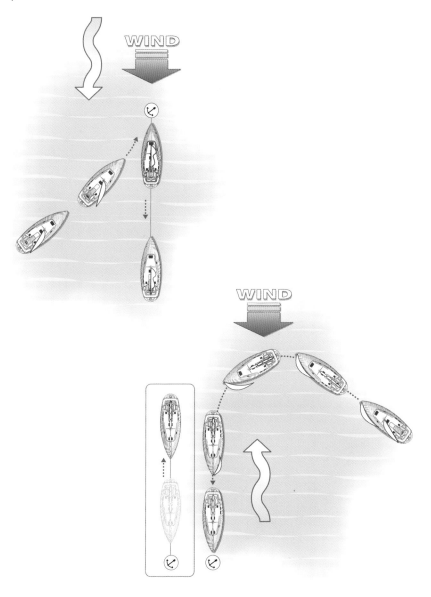

Don't forget to put up the anchor ball. If anchoring at night, a white all round light is required.

When raising the anchor, get the crew pointing in the direction of the anchor and then motor slowly ahead as they pull in the slack on the chain. Use the engine to counteract the tidal stream. Too fast and the boat will override the chain; too slow and it will be very heavy work to pull in the chain. The anchor will not come free until the chain is almost vertical. As the anchor comes to the surface, continue to motor slowly so the anchor does not swing and hit the bow of the boat as it breaks the surface. Have a bucket and deck brush ready to clean the anchor and foredeck, then secure it before raising sails or increasing speed.

If there is a problem with lifting the anchor then try breaking it out using the engine, having secured the chain to the cleat.

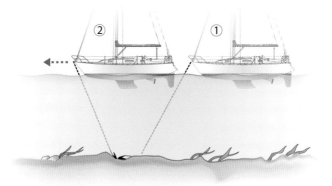

When working with the anchor and chain it is important to be aware of the weight that can be involved, even when a windlass is used.

Navigation & Tides

Chart Features

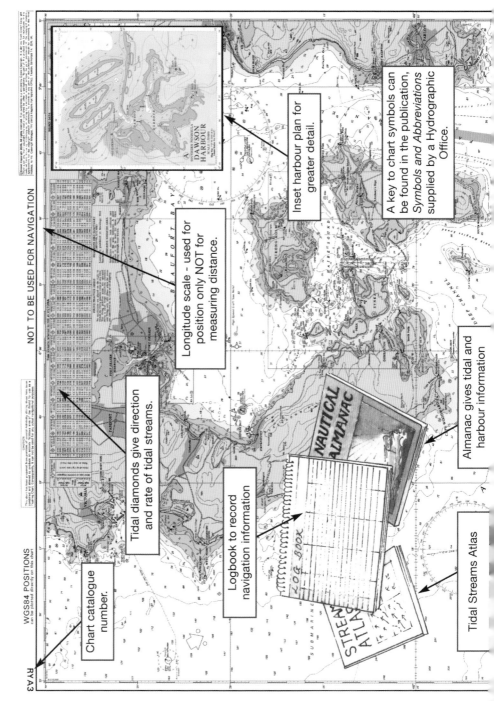

A key to chart symbols can be found in the publication, *Symbols and Abbreviations* supplied by a Hydrographic Office.

Inset harbour plan for greater detail.

Longitude scale – used for position only NOT for measuring distance.

Almanac gives tidal and harbour information

Tidal diamonds give direction and rate of tidal streams.

Logbook to record navigation information

Tidal Streams Atlas

Chart catalogue number.

NOT TO BE USED FOR NAVIGATION

WGS84 POSITIONS

RYA 3

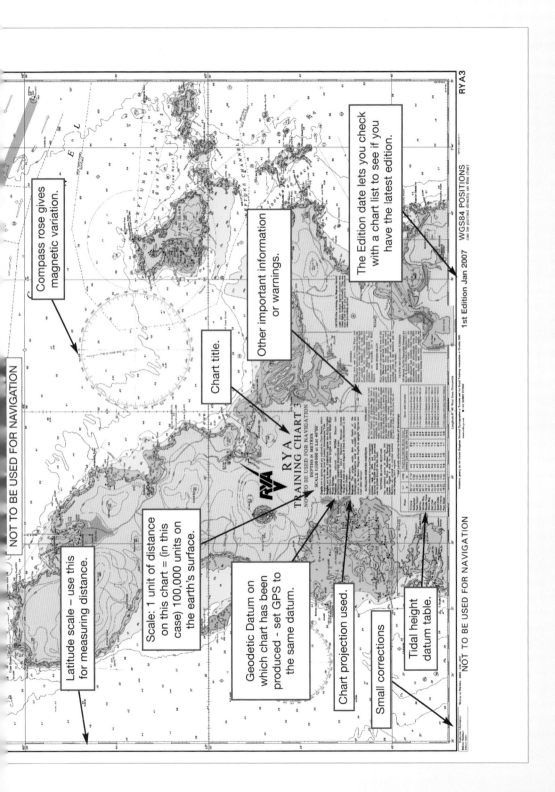

Chart Symbols

	Power transmission line with pylons and safe overhead clearance		Church		Drying contour LW line, Chart Datum
	Vertical clearance above Highest Astronomical Tide		Radio mast, television mast		Below 5m blue ribbon or differing blue tints may be shown
			Monument (including column, pillar, obelisk, statue)		Anchoring prohibited
	Harbourmaster's office		Chimney		
	Custom office		Wind motor Windfarm		Marine Farm
	Health Office, Quarantine		Tanks		Wreck, depth unknown, danger to navigation
	Post office		Recommended anchorage		Wreck, depth unknown, no danger to navigation
	Yacht Harbour, Marina		Rescue station, lifeboat station, rocket station		Wreck, depth obtained by sounding
	Radio reporting point		Fishing harbour		Wreck, swept by wire to the depth shown
	Direction of buoyage		Fishing prohibited		Submarine cable
	Mooring buoy		Perch, stake - port and starboard hand		Buried pipeline
	Wreck showing any part at level of chart datum		Pilot boarding		Overfalls, tide rips and races
	Quarry or mine		Emergency RDF station		Limit of safety zone around offshore installation
	Rock which covers and uncovers, height above Chart Datum		Marsh		Major light
	Rock awash at level of Chart Datum		Kelp		Dangerous underwater rock of unknown depth
	Visitors' Berth		Crane		Dangerous underwater rock of known depth
	Fuel station (Petrol, Diesel)		Inn and Restaurant		Caravan site Camping site
	Public slipway		Public toilets		Public telephone
	Water tap		Public car park		Bird sanctuary
	Public landing, steps, ladder		Laundrette		Coastguard Station
			Yacht Club, Sailing Club		Radar Transponder Beacon with Morse identification and Radar band

Latitude is measured north or south of the Equator.

Longitude is measured east or west from the Greenwich Meridian.

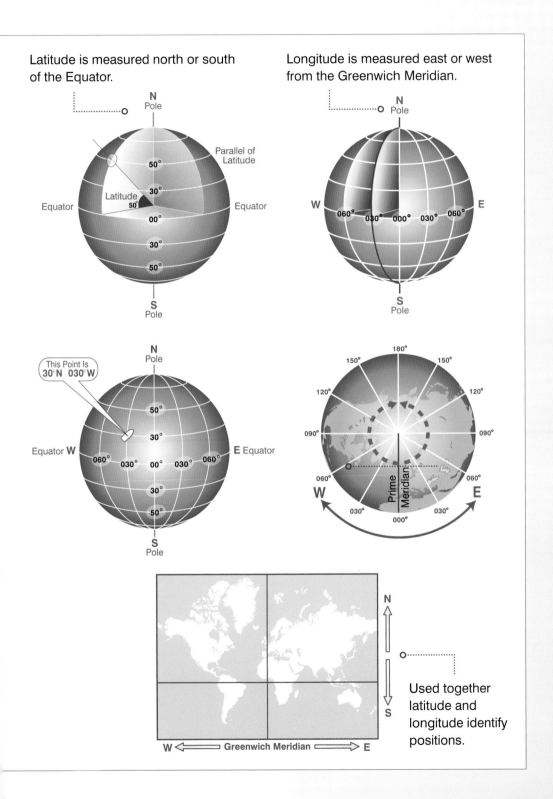

Used together latitude and longitude identify positions.

Measuring the Route

> 1 (minute) of Latitude = 1 sea mile.

For most practical purposes, distance is measured from the latitude scale, assuming that one minute of latitude equals one nautical mile. When the direction is measured off the chart it is in degrees true, °(T), because charts are produced to true north, but the boat's steering compass will point to magnetic north. The angular difference between true and magnetic north is the variation. It is caused by the world's magnetic field and it varies from place to place in the world, and can be east or west depending on the position relative to magnetic north.

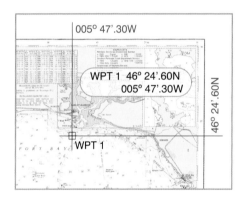

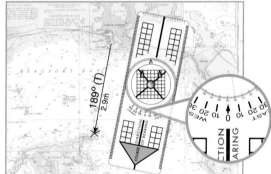

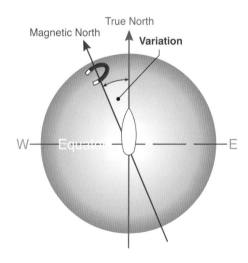

Check the variation on the chart on ⋯⋯⋯⋯⋯○
the compass rose, and then add or
subtract it to convert from true to
magnetic or vice versa every time
before plotting or steering a course.

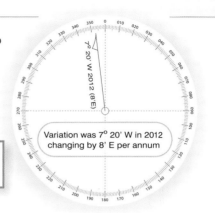

Variation was 7° 20' W in 2012
changing by 8' E per annum

189° (T) + 7° west variation = 196° (M)

Deviation, from the boat's magnetic field, can also affect the steering compass.
The engine, metal objects, mobile phones, speakers and electronic equipment
can all be the cause of deviation. It is possible to check for this on a transit or
to have the compass professionally swung. Deviation will be different on each
compass and can also be east or west.

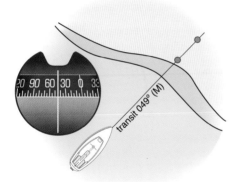

Example of a
deviation card

True bearing from chart 042° **(T)**
Variation   +7° West (applied)
Magnetic   049° **(M)**
Deviation   -4° East (applied)
Compass   045° **(C)**

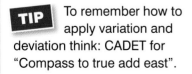

TIP To remember how to
apply variation and
deviation think: CADET for
"Compass to true add east".

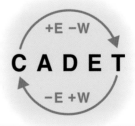

+E −W

C A D E T

−E +W

Instruments used for Navigation on the Boat

The boat will need a steering compass, with illumination for night sailing, positioned so it is clearly visible to the helmsman. Using plastic covers will protect the compass and other instruments from UV damage when they are not in use. Serious damage can make instruments impossible to read.

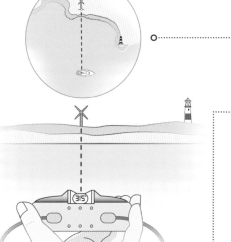

Having a hand-bearing compass is important for taking bearings to fix position, for pilotage and to assess risk of collision.

A log will show the speed and distance sailed through the water, usually measured by a paddle wheel impeller through the hull. Impellers need to be cleaned regularly to avoid fouling with weed and barnacles, which will reduce the accuracy or cause it to stop working altogether.

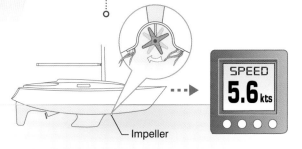

Impeller

SPEED
5.6 kts

An echo sounder uses a sound wave transducer to measure the depth of water and can be calibrated to show depth of water below the waterline or beneath the keel. Most have alarms with both shallow and deep settings, which can also be very useful for navigation.

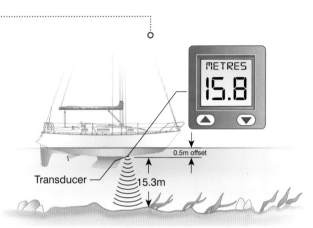

Total depth of water =15.8m

A GPS uses signals from satellites to fix the position very accurately and display it as latitude and longitude. It is essentially a position fixing device but from the continually updated position it can calculate and display the course and speed over the ground (COG and SOG). COG and SOG include the effect of tidal stream and leeway, whereas the compass and log can only show the course and speed through the water. Even a small, inexpensive handheld set will have these features, but a built-in set will have a bigger screen and more reliable power supply, but will require an externally mounted aerial. The position information from the GPS can be interfaced into the VHF/DSC or other equipment.

A GPS set can use waypoints (WPT) for navigation. A WPT is a position chosen by the navigator, often as part of a route. Its latitude and longitude is measured off the chart or found in a book and programmed into the GPS, which will then display the direction and distance to it. Waypoints can also be used to guide the boat into a harbour or avoid a hazard. The distance and direction displayed by the GPS needs to be checked against that measured off the chart, as inputting errors are easy to make. Checking that the route is safe is the navigator's responsibility. The GPS will calculate the direct line from one WPT to the next, taking no account of hazards such as rocks, sandbanks or even land. Consider that in a very busy area many boats may be using the same WPT and in poor visibility or at night it might be better to put the WPT adjacent to the buoy to avoid getting too close.

The direction to the WPT displayed on the GPS will not take into account the tidal stream. The navigator must calculate a course to steer to counteract any effect. If no allowance is made for tidal stream, the direction to the WPT will continually change as the boat is taken sideways; it will have to sail further and may even be put into danger. To help monitor any drift the GPS has a cross-track error feature, shown as XTE, which shows how far off the original track the boat has drifted. This is excellent for monitoring progress on the calculated course to steer. The GPS will provide an ETA as well.

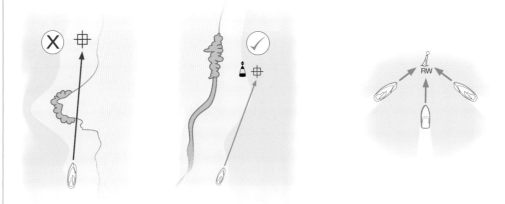

Dedicated electronic chart plotters are an alternative way of navigating. They display the chart on a screen and can be interfaced with a GPS, making it possible for the position to be shown on the chart. They can store tidal data and do navigational calculations. Electronic charts can also be displayed on a computer screen.

Electronic charts on disc and cartridge come in two main types:

■ Raster charts look identical to their paper equivalents because they are a scanned version of the chart. If the zoom function is overused on raster charts the image goes out of focus, like putting a page too close to your eyes

■ Vector charts are produced with layers of information that can be selected or deselected as required. The charts can also be interrogated for more information and hazard warning lines set up. These charts may look different from the familiar paper chart but are more adaptable in use.

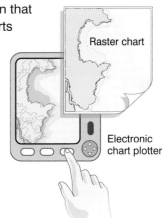

Raster chart

Electronic chart plotter

Like all charts, electronic charts require updating which may mean buying a new disc.

Tides: The Basics

Tides are caused by the gravitational pull of the sun and the moon. When the sun and moon are in line the effect is greatest, giving spring tides, and the difference between high water and low water is most extreme. When the sun and moon are at right angles neap tides are the result. The moon takes a lunar month, 28 days, to orbit the earth, giving a pattern of movement between neaps and springs of about seven days.

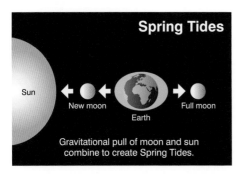

Spring Tides

Sun   New moon   Earth   Full moon

Gravitational pull of moon and sun combine to create Spring Tides.

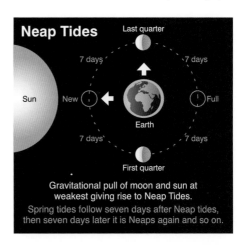

Neap Tides   Last quarter

7 days   7 days

Sun   New   Earth   Full

7 days   7 days

First quarter

Gravitational pull of moon and sun at weakest giving rise to Neap Tides.
Spring tides follow seven days after Neap tides, then seven days later it is Neaps again and so on.

There are usually two high waters (HW) and two low waters (LW) per day, each just over six hours apart. The difference in height between high water and low water is called the range of the tide, with spring tides giving the maximum range and neap tides the minimum.

Add one hour in the non-shaded area to convert to summer time (DST).

The height of tide given in tide tables is a prediction, which can be influenced by the barometric pressure and weather conditions. High pressure reduces the height and low pressure and storm surges have the opposite effect.

TIME ZONE UT
For Summer Time add ONE hour in **non-shaded areas**

SPRING & NEAP TIDES
Dates in red are SPRINGS
Dates in blue are NEAPS

TIMES AND HEIGHTS OF HIGH AND LOW WATERS

SEPTEMBER

Day	Time	m		Day	Time	m
1 SU	0501	3.4		16 M	0712	3.5
	1006	2.0			1225	1.9
	1737	3.5			1945	3.6
	2259	2.0				
2 M	0631	3.4		17 TU	0113	1.7
	1149	2.1			0832	3.7
	1904	3.5			1347	1.8
					2052	3.7
3 TU	0046	1.8		18 W	0220	1.5
	0754	3.6			0925	3.9
	1321	1.9			1445	1.5
	2016	3.7			2138	3.9
4 W	0156	1.5		19 TH	0309	1.3
	0856	3.8			1006	4.0
	1422	1.5			1529	1.4
	2110	3.9			2216	4.0
5 TH	0251	1.2		20 F	0350	1.1
	0944	4.0			1041	4.1
	1513	1.3			1608	1.1
	2155	4.0			2248	4.0
6 F	0340	0.9		21 SA	0427	0.9
	1026	4.2			1112	4.1
	1602	0.9			1644	1.0
	2236	4.2		O	2317	4.0
7 SA	0427	0.6		22 SU	0502	0.8
	1107	4.3			1139	4.1
	1650	0.7			1717	0.9
●	2318	4.3			2343	4.0
8 SU	0513	0.4		23 M	0533	0.8
	1149	4.4			1209	4.1
	1732	0.6			1747	1.0
9 M	0003	4.4		24 TU	0015	4.0
	0554	0.4			0601	0.9
	1238	4.4			1239	4.0
	1814	0.5			1812	1.0
10 TU	0053	4.4		25 W	0049	4.0
	0634	0.4			0624	1.0
	1326	4.4			1311	4.0
	1854	0.6			1835	1.1
11 W	0142	4.3		26 TH	0123	4.0
	0715	0.6			0646	1.1
	1412	4.3			1342	4.0
	1936	0.7			1900	1.2
12 TH	0232	4.1		27 F	0156	3.9
	0756	0.8			0712	1.3
	1500	4.1			1413	3.9
	2018	1.0			1928	1.4
13 F	0323	4.0		28 SA	0232	3.8
	0840	1.2			0743	1.6
	1550	4.0			1450	3.7
	2108	1.4			2005	1.6
14 SA	0421	3.7		29 SU	0317	3.7
	0935	1.5			0825	1.8
	1649	3.7			1539	3.7
	2211	1.6			2056	1.9
15 SU	0536	3.6		30 M	0425	3.6
	1049	1.8			0931	2.1
	1812	3.6			1653	3.5
	2340	1.8			2222	2.0

OCTOBER

Day	Time	m		Day	Time	m
1 TU	0600	3.4		16 W	0047	1.9
	1123	2.2			0811	3.7
	1830	3.5			1324	1.9
					2032	3.7
2 W	0020	1.9		17 TH	0154	1.6
	0730	3.6			0901	3.9
	1300	1.9			1418	1.6
	1950	3.7			2116	3.8
3 TH	0134	1.5		18 F	0239	1.4
	0834	3.8			0940	4.0
	1402	1.5			1459	1.4
	2048	3.9			2152	3.9
4 F	0229	1.2		19 SA	0319	1.2
	0922	4.0			1013	4.1
	1452	1.2			1537	1.2
	2133	4.1			2222	4.0
5 SA	0316	0.8		20 SU	0355	1.0
	1004	4.3			1042	4.1
	1539	0.9			1613	1.0
	2216	4.3			2250	4.0
6 SU	0403	0.6		21 M	0430	0.9
	1045	4.4			1108	4.1
	1625	0.6			1646	1.0
●	2258	4.4		O	2317	4.0
7 M	0450	0.4		22 TU	0503	0.9
	1126	4.5			1135	4.1
	1710	0.5			1717	1.0
	2340	4.4			2345	4.0
8 TU	0531	0.4		23 W	0530	1.0
	1210	4.5			1205	4.1
	1752	0.5			1744	1.0
9 W	0028	4.4		24 TH	0020	4.0
	0611	0.5			0556	1.0
	1258	4.4			1237	4.0
	1832	0.6			1807	1.1
10 TH	0118	4.4		25 F	0054	4.0
	0650	0.7			0619	1.2
	1344	4.3			1308	4.0
	1911	0.8			1833	1.2
11 F	0208	4.2		26 SA	0129	4.0
	0731	1.0			0646	1.4
	1431	4.1			1342	4.0
	1954	1.1			1903	1.4
12 SA	0259	4.0		27 SU	0208	3.9
	0817	1.4			0721	1.5
	1521	3.9			1420	3.8
	2041	1.4			1942	1.5
13 SU	0359	3.7		28 M	0257	3.7
	0912	1.7			0805	1.8
	1619	3.7			1512	3.7
	2145	1.7			2036	1.8
14 M	0515	3.6		29 TU	0405	3.6
	1028	2.0			0913	2.1
	1744	3.5			1626	3.6
	2314	1.9			2157	1.9
15 TU	0657	3.6		30 W	0534	3.6
	1202	2.0			1053	2.1
	1927	3.5			1758	3.5
					2340	1.8
				31 TH	0702	3.7
					1226	1.9
					1920	3.7

NOVEMBER

Day	Time	m		Day	Time	m
1 F	0059	1.5		16 SA	0156	1.5
	0806	3.9			0903	4.0
	1331	1.5			1422	1.5
	2020	3.9			2117	3.7
2 SA	0157	1.2		17 SU	0237	1.4
	0855	4.1			0937	4.0
	1424	1.2			1500	1.4
	2108	4.1			2149	3.9
3 SU	0247	0.9		18 M	0315	1.2
	0938	4.4			1007	4.0
	1512	0.9			1536	1.2
	2153	4.3			2220	4.0
4 M	0336	0.7		19 TU	0354	1.1
	1022	4.4			1035	4.1
	1600	0.7			1614	1.1
●	2237	4.4			2250	4.0
5 TU	0422	0.5		20 W	0430	1.1
	1103	4.5			1105	4.1
	1647	0.6			1648	1.1
	2321	4.4		O	2321	4.0
6 W	0508	0.5		21 TH	0502	1.1
	1144	4.5			1135	4.1
	1730	0.6			1718	1.1
					2355	4.0
7 TH	0008	4.4		22 F	0530	1.2
	0548	0.7			1209	4.1
	1232	4.4			1747	1.1
	1811	0.7				
8 F	0058	4.4		23 SA	0033	4.0
	0629	0.9			0600	1.3
	1318	4.3			1245	4.0
	1851	0.9			1818	1.2
9 SA	0147	4.2		24 SU	0113	4.0
	0710	1.1			0632	1.4
	1405	4.1			1323	4.0
	1934	1.2			1852	1.3
10 SU	0239	4.0		25 M	0156	4.0
	0756	1.4			0711	1.5
	1454	3.9			1406	3.9
	2020	1.4			1935	1.4
11 M	0338	3.8		26 TU	0248	3.8
	0850	1.7			0800	1.7
	1550	3.7			1459	3.7
	2118	1.7			2029	1.5
12 TU	0449	3.7		27 W	0352	3.7
	0957	2.0			0903	1.8
	1704	3.5			1606	3.7
	2230	1.9			2136	1.6
13 W	0620	3.6		28 TH	0510	3.7
	1120	2.1			1019	1.9
	1842	3.4			1726	3.7
	2356	1.9			2254	1.6
14 TH	0731	3.7		29 F	0630	3.8
	1240	1.9			1140	1.7
	1952	3.5			1845	3.7
15 F	0106	1.7		30 SA	0011	1.4
	0822	3.8			0733	4.0
	1337	1.7			1252	1.5
	2040	3.7			1948	3.9

DECEMBER

Day	Time	m		Day	Time	m
1 SU	0117	1.3		16 M	0149	1.6
	0826	4.1			0852	3.9
	1352	1.3			1419	1.5
	2043	4.0			2110	3.7
2 M	0215	1.1		17 TU	0235	1.4
	0915	4.3			0929	4.0
	1446	1.0			1502	1.4
	2133	4.1			2149	3.8
3 TU	0307	0.9		18 W	0318	1.4
	1000	4.4			1005	4.0
	1538	0.8			1542	1.3
	2221	4.3			2226	3.9
4 W	0358	0.8		19 TH	0358	1.3
	1043	4.4			1039	4.0
	1627	0.7			1621	1.1
●	2306	4.3			2301	4.0
5 TH	0447	0.8		20 F	0437	1.2
	1126	4.4			1113	4.1
	1715	0.7			1700	1.1
	2352	4.3			2337	4.0
6 F	0531	0.9		21 SA	0513	1.2
	1210	4.4			1147	4.1
	1757	0.8			1734	1.0
7 SA	0042	4.3		22 SU	0018	4.1
	0613	1.0			0548	1.2
	1257	4.2			1228	4.0
	1837	0.9			1811	1.0
8 SU	0132	4.2		23 M	0102	4.1
	0654	1.2			0627	1.3
	1343	4.0			1311	4.0
	1918	1.1			1849	1.0
9 M	0222	4.0		24 TU	0149	4.0
	0737	1.4			0708	1.3
	1430	3.9			1357	4.0
	2000	1.4			1933	1.1
10 TU	0314	3.9		25 W	0239	4.0
	0824	1.6			0756	1.4
	1520	3.7			1450	3.9
	2047	1.5			2022	1.2
11 W	0412	3.7		26 TH	0338	4.0
	0918	1.9			0850	1.5
	1617	3.6			1549	3.8
	2141	1.7			2116	1.3
12 TH	0517	3.7		27 F	0442	3.9
	1021	2.0			0949	1.5
	1723	3.4			1656	3.7
	2244	1.8			2215	1.4
13 F	0624	3.7		28 SA	0552	3.9
	1134	2.0			1057	1.6
	1835	3.4			1810	3.7
	2355	1.8			2325	1.4
14 SA	0721	3.7		29 SU	0658	3.9
	1241	1.9			1212	1.5
	1937	3.5			1917	3.7
15 SU	0058	1.7		30 M	0038	1.4
	0810	3.8			0758	4.0
	1334	1.7			1323	1.4
	2028	3.6			2021	3.8
				31 TU	0147	1.3
					0853	4.1
					1426	1.2
					2118	4.0

Tidal Terms

The depths shown on the chart are the charted depths, the amount of water below chart datum. Chart datum is approximately the same as the lowest astronomical tide, and is the lowest the water is ever likely to be. The areas shown in green on the chart are drying heights, with the underlined figures showing the height above chart datum.

MHWS	Mean High Water Springs
HAT	Highest Astronomical Tide
MHWN	Mean High Water Neaps
MLWN	Mean Low Water Neaps
MLWS	Mean Low Water Springs
CD	Charted Depth

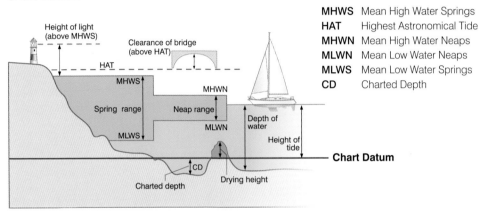

As the tide rises and falls the depth of water over charted depths and drying heights changes, but it is never less than shown on the chart, except under exceptional circumstances.

Depth of water = height of tide + charted depth

Or

Depth of water = height of tide - drying height

Tide tables show the time and height of the tide at high water and low water for standard ports, and the differences to add or subtract to convert the data to the secondary ports nearby.

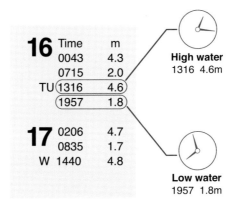

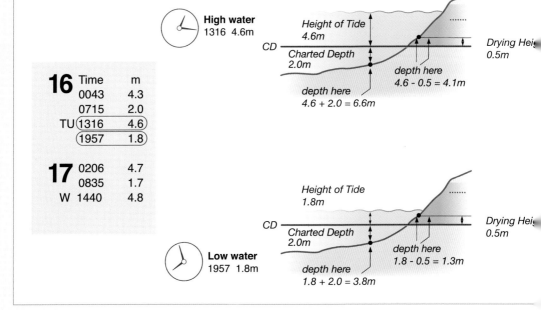

Tidal Streams

The tidal stream, which is the horizontal movement of the water, affects both the speed of the boat and its course.

The log shows the speed through the water, and this may be increased or decreased by the tidal stream. It is the resulting speed over the ground which determines when the boat will arrive.

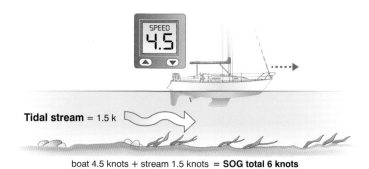

boat 4.5 knots + stream 1.5 knots = **SOG total 6 knots**

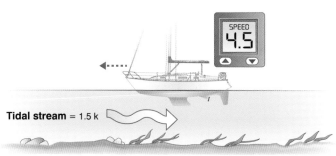

boat 4.5 knots - stream 1.5 knots = **SOG total 3 knots**

Similarly, if the course through the water that the boat is steering means there is a sideways tidal stream the course over the ground will be different.

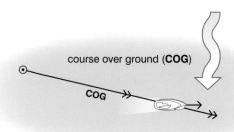

Estimated position (EP)

This tidal stream effect is drawn on the chart when plotting an estimated position (EP).

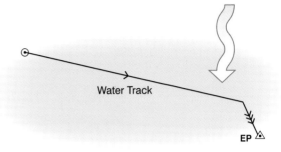

Water Track

EP

Course to steer (CTS)

When calculating a course to steer (CTS) the tidal stream must be taken into consideration from the start.

Course over ground (COG)

Tide

Course to steer (CTS)

Tidal streams also need to be considered when planning a passage.
The information on tidal streams for navigation or passage planning is found from the tidal diamonds on the charts, in a tidal stream atlas or in the almanac.

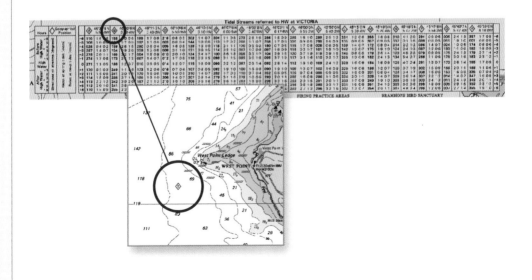

Tidal Stream Atlas

The atlas gives a clear display of the pattern during the day, especially useful when passage planning.

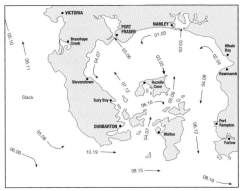

1 hour after HW Victoria

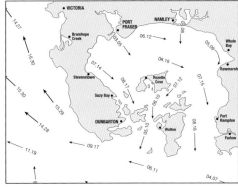

2 hours after HW Victoria

The tidal streams influence the sea state as well. If the wind is against the tidal stream the conditions will be far rougher than if wind and tide are together.

Additionally, in some places where the depth changes suddenly the tidal stream can cause increased turbulence. These areas of overfalls are often shown on the chart.

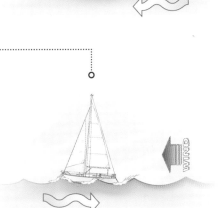

The Passage Plan:
Itchenham, in Namley Harbour towards Rozelle Cove

All the examples for passage planning, navigation and pilotage are from the RYA charts and RYA Training Almanac used on shorebased courses since 2006, and available from the RYA and RYA Training Centres.

The passage:

From Itchenham Boatyard towards Rozelle Cove on August 9th on a 9 metre yacht with a crew of 2 adults.

The boat is moored on the pontoon outside the boatyard, which dried 1.0m according to the almanac.

The boat has a draught of 1.6m and an average cruising speed of 5 knots.

The weather has been checked and it will be possible to update the forecast during the passage from the Coastguard broadcasts.

Details of the plan will be left with friends ashore.

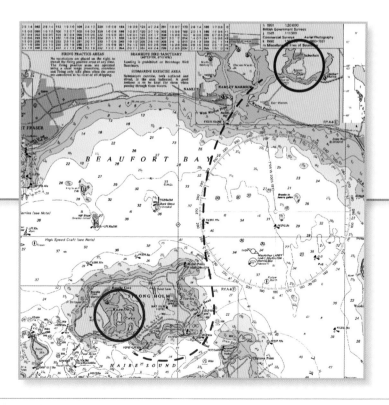

Making a Plan

Start by collecting basic data from the almanac:

- High water and low water at the reference port(s) for the tidal stream atlas and for the tidal diamonds on all the charts that will be used for the planning and the passage

- High water and low water at the ports of departure and arrival, and anywhere that might be in the contingency plan to calculate any problem with departure and entry times.

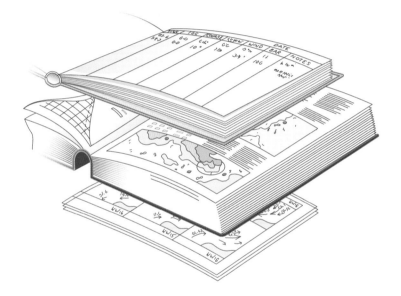

	HW	HW	LW
Victoria	1137 DST	5.5m	0.8m
Namley Harbour	1308 DST	3.9m	0.3m
Port Fraser	1303 DST	4.1m	0.4m

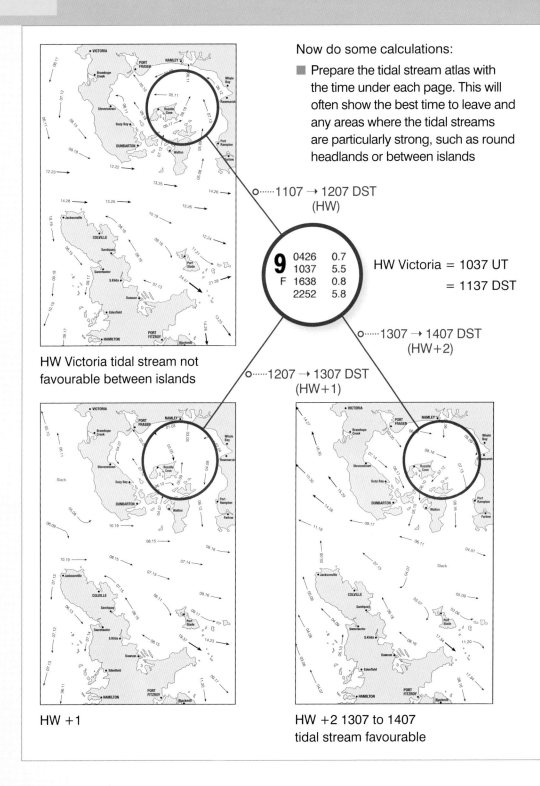

Now do some calculations:

▨ Prepare the tidal stream atlas with the time under each page. This will often show the best time to leave and any areas where the tidal streams are particularly strong, such as round headlands or between islands

○⋯⋯1107 → 1207 DST
(HW)

9
F
0426	0.7
1037	5.5
1638	0.8
2252	5.8

HW Victoria = 1037 UT
= 1137 DST

○⋯⋯1307 → 1407 DST
(HW+2)

○⋯⋯1207 → 1307 DST
(HW+1)

HW Victoria tidal stream not favourable between islands

HW +1

HW +2 1307 to 1407
tidal stream favourable

■ Find the range of the tide (HW height - LW height). Compare it to the mean range to find a spring, neap or in-between

Victoria: 5.5m - 0.8m = 4.7m.   Spring range 4.9m, so close to springs for Tidal Stream data

■ Calculate high water and low water at any secondary ports

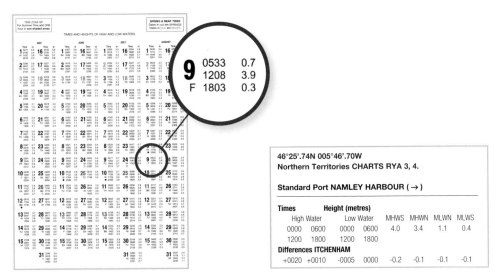

46°25'.74N 005°46'.70W
Northern Territories CHARTS RYA 3, 4.

Standard Port NAMLEY HARBOUR (→)

Times	Height (metres)					
High Water		Low Water		MHWS	MHWN	MLWN	MLWS
0000	0600	0000	0600	4.0	3.4	1.1	0.4
1200	1800	1200	1800				
Differences ITCHENHAM							
+0020	+0010	-0005	0000	-0.2	-0.1	-0.1	-0.1

■ High and low water times for Namley Harbour on 9 August

■ Differences for Itchenham

	HW	LW	HW	LW
Namley Harbour	1208 UT	0.7m	3.9m	0.3m
Correction for Itchenham	+20 mins.	- 0.1m	- 0.2m	- 0.1m
Correction for DST	+1 hour			
Itchenham	**1328 DST**	**0.6m**	**3.7m**	**0.2m**

■ Add the hour to convert to DST after calculating the correction for the secondary port

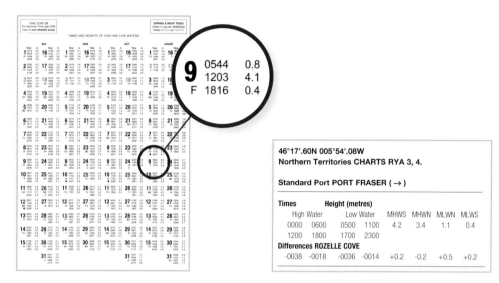

46°17'.60N 005°54'.08W
Northern Territories CHARTS RYA 3, 4.

Standard Port PORT FRASER (→)

Times		Height (metres)					
High Water		Low Water		MHWS	MHWN	MLWN	MLWS
0000	0600	0500	1100	4.2	3.4	1.1	0.4
1200	1800	1700	2300				
Differences ROZELLE COVE							
-0038	-0018	-0036	-0014	+0.2	-0.2	+0.5	+0.2

■ High and low water times for Port Fraser on 9 August

■ Differences for Rozelle Cove

	HW	HW	LW
Port Fraser	1203 UT	4.1m	0.4m
Correction for Rozelle Cove	- 38 mins.	+ 0.2m	+ 0.2m
Correction for DST	+ 1 hour		
Rozelle Cove	**1225 DST**	**4.3m**	**0.6m**

■ Use the secondary port information to calculate when it is possible to leave and arrive in relation to the depth of water. Check on the chart for depth information and notes. Read the pilotage notes in the almanac and pilot books for advice.

> Depth of water - draught = clearance

When can the Boat Leave?

HW height at Itchenham	3.7m
Berth dries	- 1.0m
Depth on berth at HW	**2.7m**
Draught of boat	- 1.6m
Clearance under keel at HW	1.1m

At HW the clearance will be 1.1m, but the boat could leave earlier or later with less clearance if that would be more convenient. The skipper must decide the minimum clearance acceptable. Consider whether the conditions are likely to be rough, the nature of the seabed and if the tide will be rising or falling. Going aground an hour before HW, on mud, is definitely not as serious as an hour after HW on something much harder.

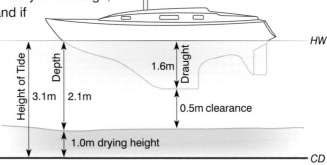

Calculate the height of tide required

Draught of yacht	1.6m	
Chosen clearance	0.5m	
	2.1m	
Charted information	dries 1.0m	+(drying height above chart datum so add)
Height of tide required	**3.1m**	

The tidal curve diagram can be used to calculate the earliest or latest time before or after HW that the boat can leave with the acceptable clearance. Work out first the height of tide required, taking into account the draught of the boat and the depth shown on the chart.

(If there is a charted depth shown then deduct it to get the height of tide required.)

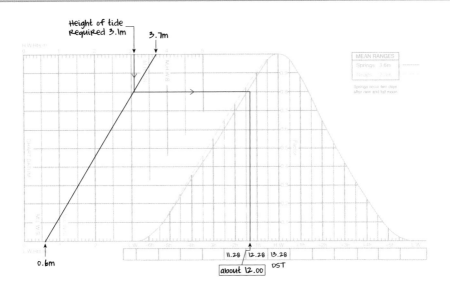

Height of tide Required 3.1m — 3.7m

MEAN RANGES
Springs 3.6m

Springs occur two days after new and full moon

0.6m

11.28 / 12.28 13.28
about 12.00 DST

When is the earliest time before HW that the boat can leave the pontoon?

Use the tidal curve for the standard port, Namley Harbour, with the tidal data for the secondary port, Itchenham. Use the LW height before HW and the springs curve, in this case.

- Enter HW time and fill in the boxes for each hour before HW
- Mark in the height of HW and LW and draw a line between them
- Find 3.1m on the HW height scale
- Draw a line down to the HW/LW line, across to the curve and then down to find the earliest time before HW. Use the spring curve in this case
- The earliest time to leave is about 1200

Don't forget to consider the depth at the port of arrival too.

The minimum depth in Rozelle Marina at LW will be:

LW height Rozelle Cove	0.6m
Charted depth in marina	+ 3.0m
Depth of water at LW	**3.6m**
Draught of the boat	- 1.6m
Clearance	2.0m

With a minimum clearance of 2.0m at LW it is possible to enter the marina at any time which will not complicate the plan. If departure or arrival time is limited or does not fit in with other considerations, there are different ways to solve this problem, such as anchoring and waiting for the tide.

■ Look for a tidal gate. This is a point that must be reached by a certain time because of the strength of the tidal stream or insufficient tidal height. These can be headlands, between islands or shallow areas. The tidal stream between the islands can be 2 knots, so aim to do that part of the passage with a south-going tidal stream. The tidal stream atlas shows when this will occur.

■ Tidal stream information in the atlas or for the diamonds on the chart is shown in hours before and after HW, with the actual time being taken as the middle of the hour. Work it out as in the table, which can then be used during the passage to look up the correct hour to use. On different charts the reference port for the tidal stream can change. Always check this for every chart at the passage planning stage and prepare a table of hours for each.

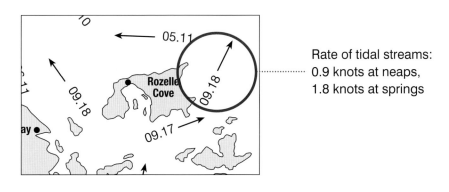

Rate of tidal streams:
0.9 knots at neaps,
1.8 knots at springs

	0907 to 1007 = - 2 hours
	1007 to 1107 = - 1 hour before HW
HW Victoria **1137 DST** =	**1107 to 1207 = HW hour**
	1207 to 1307 = + 1 hour after HW
	1307 to 1407 = + 2 hours
	1407 to 1507 = + 3 hours
	1507 to 1607 = + 4 hours

NAMLEY HARBOUR - Standard Port

46°25'.74N 005°46'.70W
Northern Territories CHARTS RYA 3, 4.

Standard Port NAMLEY HARBOUR (→)

Times				Height (metres)			
High Water		Low Water		MHWS	MHWN	MLWN	MLWS
0000	0600	0000	0600	4.0	3.4	1.1	0.4
1200	1800	1200	1800				
Differences ITCHENHAM							
+0020	+0010	-0005	0000	-0.2	-0.1	-0.1	-0.1
Differences EMSBOURNE							
+0010	+0010	-0010	-0005	-0.3	-0.1	0.0	-0.1

DESCRIPTION. The harbour provides very good shelter in the various channels, creeks and marinas. There are five marinas and numerous visitors moorings along the channels. Hbr speed limit of 8kn. Hbr staff do prosecute for speeding offences, they also prosecute sailing vessels for failing to display a motoring cone when motor sailing.

APPROACH WAYPOINT. 46°24'.41N 005°47'.08W.

PILOTAGE NOTES. APPROACHES: Leave the Bar Beacon [Fl(2)R.10s14m2M] (R bn) 50m to port, the channel N'ward is only 100m wide. It is advisable to select a transit ahead to check for drift to avoid being swept onto the shoals that flank the entrance. Leaving the tide gauge (Q.G) to stbd make towards the SCM where the channel divides N towards Emsbourne and ENE towards Itchenham. Depths may change in this area and the buoys will be moved accordingly; the HM should be consulted for the latest information. Both main channels are well marked with buoys. Do not enter or leave harbour during onshore gales as dangerous conditions may be encountered especially with a spring ebb.

TIDAL STREAMS AND HEIGHTS. Best entry/exit is HW -3 to HW +1 avoiding the confused seas caused by the strong ebb stream. During spring tides, the bar becomes very uncomfortable in onshore winds > F5 combined with the ebb stream. The bar is dredged to 1.5m below CD but this may vary by ±0.75m after heavy onshore gales.

LIGHTS AND MARKS. Namley Bar Beacon [Fl(2) R.10s14m2M] is a conspicuous red painted wooden structure. A weather station on the beacon www. namleymetstn.co.nt gives access to the current weather conditions in the vicinity of the entrance. All channels within the harbour are well marked by day. Emsbourne and Namley Channels are partly lit. Nutworth Channel and Itchenham Reach are unlit.

VHF RADIO. Namley Harbour Radio and patrol vessels VHF Ch **14**, 16. Marinas VHF Ch 80.

FACILITIES. Clockwise from W Warren Point.
Namley Marina. 30 V. Access at all states of the tide via dredged channel 2m; pontoons have 1.6m. ME, EL, P, D, M, Gas, CH, C (25 tonnes). From Bone Point SC follow marked channel to marina. **North Namley Yacht Haven.** 20 V. 1.3m channel to marina. Access HW -5 to +4½ ME, EL, FW, BH (10 tonnes). **Emsbourne Marina.** 10 V. Approach channel dries 0.5m. Access HW ±2 over 1.0m sill, which maintains 1.7m inside. Slip, FW, Gas, CH, ME, EL, BH (60 tonnes), C (20 tonnes). **Nutworth Marina.** 6 V. Drying 0.5m in approach channel and berths. FW, P&D (cans), Bar, R. There is a public slipway at Nutworth SC. **Chidham Marina.** 20 V. Enter well marked channel to lock. Channel is dredged to CD. A waiting pontoon is outside the lock. Call Lock Keeper on Ch 80 and await G light. Free flow near HW times. **Itchenham.** Unmarked channel, stay close to moored vessels. AB (drying 1.0m), FW, BY, ME, EL, BH (10 tonnes), Slip.

▥ Read the details of the ports of departure and arrival. Look for restriction on entering/leaving which are significant when fixing a departure time. Check tidal streams, tidal heights, lock or bridge opening times and consider if sunrise and sunset are important. Arriving in the dark at new destination and at the end of a long passage can be hard work for the skipper. Make the detailed pilotage plan later with details of buoyage, local regulations, VHF calling channels, speed limits, recommended routes and facilities

▥ The simplest way of calculating approximate passage time is obviously distance divided by average speed. Including the increase of speed expected from the tidal stream will increase the accuracy. Look at the strengths of the tidal streams shown in the atlas over the hours of the passage and estimate how much will be gained.

An Overview of a Skipper's
Handwritten Plan

Overview of the Plan

This is a very suitable passage for the boat and the crew.
The earliest time to leave is approximately 1200 to reach the
Namley bar Beacon at about 1300. Leaving just before HW
means the tide is not falling in the narrow creek and even
though the tidal stream will be against the boat it's not likely
to be very strong. The boat will cross the bar within the
recommended time and the tidal stream will be favourable
for the passage. The passage will take about 4 hours and
there are no constraints on entering Rozelle Cove Marina.

2

Passage Planning

Route and Waypoint Planning

1. Choose the route on a small scale chart showing the whole passage, but check on a detailed chart before making a final decision. Plot the route on the planning chart or make a plan or list.

2. Select the routing waypoints. These are just navigation marks or other turning points whose latitude and longitude have been programmed into the GPS to form the route. Calculate the direction and distance between the waypoints on the chart and check this against the information displayed by the GPS. This will show any mistakes made with measuring latitude and longitude or when inputting them into the GPS. If using waypoints from an almanac or other book check those too.

Hazards

The passage notes in the almanac mention large commercial vessels and high-speed ferries crossing the route that the yacht will take, so keeping a good lookout will be even more important than usual.

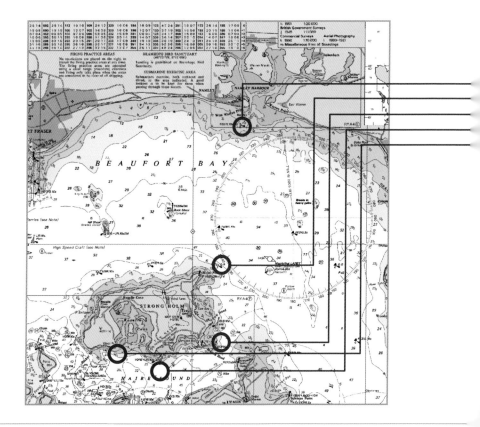

Contingency Plan

Once the boat has left it will not be able to return because of the tide. The boat could divert to Port Fraser, and other marinas are possible depending on the weather and the height of tide. Information about the passage should be left with someone onshore who knows how to inform the Coastguard if they do not hear of the boat's safe arrival.

These directions are for general information only and to check against the GPS. They are not courses to steer, as no allowance has been made for tidal stream.

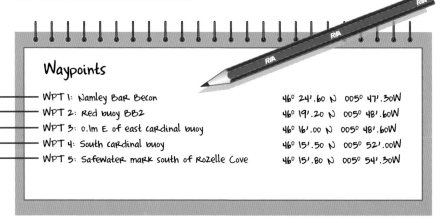

Waypoints

WPT 1: Namley Bar Becon	46° 24'.60 N 005° 47'.30W
WPT 2: Red buoy BB2	46° 19'.20 N 005° 48'.60W
WPT 3: 0.1m E of east cardinal buoy	46° 16'.00 N 005° 48'.60W
WPT 4: South cardinal buoy	46° 15'.50 N 005° 52'.00W
WPT 5: Safewater mark south of Rozelle Cove	46° 15'.80 N 005° 54'.30W

Route	Heading	Distance
WPT 1 to WPT 2	189° (T)	5.5 miles
WPT 2 to WPT 3	178° (T)	3.2 miles
WPT 3 to WPT 4	259° (T)	2.5 miles
WPT 4 to WPT 5	282° (T)	1.6 miles

Having planned the passage, the pilotage and prepared the boat, the final go / don't go decision is usually down to the weather. Consider the weather for the passage and for the return.

The navigation on the day will consist of:

- Knowing the position of the boat at all times. This can be done by:

    Observation of a charted object.

    GPS, plotting latitude and longitude or distance and direction to a waypoint.

    Taking a fix.

    Working up an estimated position (EP).

- Keeping a record in the logbook of alterations of course, the distance covered, echo sounder readings and GPS positions

- Calculating a course to steer (CTS) when necessary to the next waypoint on the route.

At the departure point, be ready with the course to steer for the helmsman and make an entry in the logbook.

How to Work out a Course to Steer (CTS)

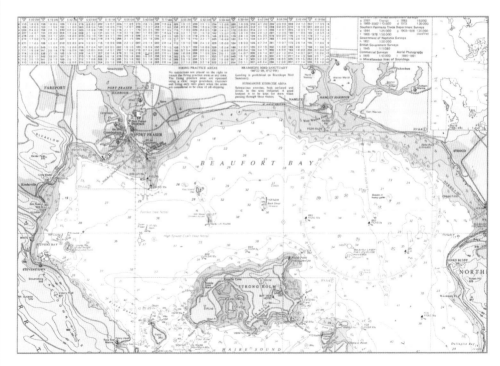

WPT 1 to WPT 2:

Calculate a course to steer to allow for the tidal stream. Use the GPS to check.

1. Plot the course over the ground (COG)
2. Measure the distance. Decide if it's a half-hour, 1 or 2-hour diagram
3. Calculate the tidal stream (TS)
4. Plot the TS from the starting position
5. Use the average speed through the water from the log and mark this distance from the end of the TS to the COG to give the course to steer (CTS). Apply variation
6. Consider leeway. Head up 5° or 10° if necessary
7. Look at the diagram for an ETA

Make a log entry for the alteration of course. En route to the buoy, monitor the boat's course over the ground. Using different functions on the GPS is an excellent way to do this.

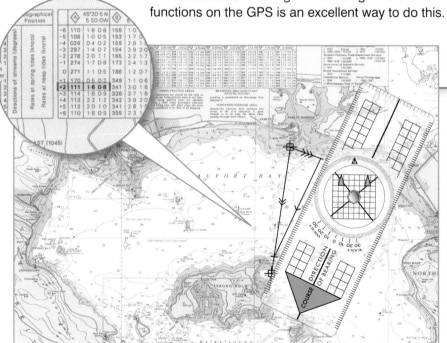

CTS = 208° (T)

7° Variation

215°(M)

If the buoy ahead has been put in as a WPT the GPS will give a continuous display of the direction and distance towards it. This will not be the same as the calculated course to steer, because the GPS does not take into account the tidal stream, but the direction will remain constant if the boat is on course.

- The cross track error function on the GPS will show if the boat drifts off the course over the ground.

- A single bearing on the beacon behind the boat or on the buoy ahead, once it is sighted, will show if the boat is off course. Compare the bearing to the course over the ground.

Between waypoints 2 and 3 the distance is much less, so use a half hour plot and, as there is no convenient tidal diamond, use the tidal atlas for tidal stream information.

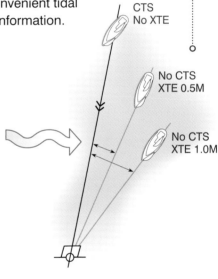

CTS
No XTE

No CTS
XTE 0.5M

No CTS
XTE 1.0M

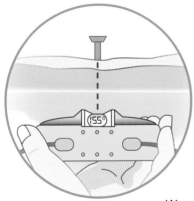

155°

Waypoint 3 is on both charts, so it is a good position to change to the more detailed chart, which shows all the buoys and the entrance to the cove. Alternatively, use a fix to do this. At waypoint 4 follow the pilotage plan.

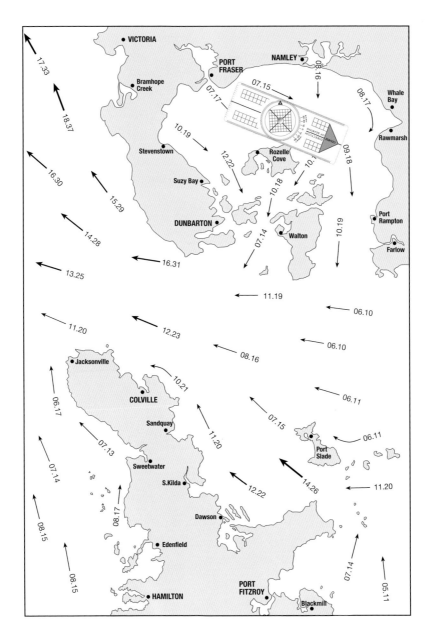

The tidal stream can be measured directly from the atlas.

On passage, the skipper needs to monitor the position. This can be done in several different ways.

■ General observations of buoys and any coastal features. Each buoy on the route confirms the position, but clearly identified features can be used to get a fix of position. Make a note in the logbook when a fix is taken, using the time when the information was recorded and not when you finished plotting it on the chart.

Three Point Fix

Identify 3 features that are on the chart, not too far away from the boat, on which to take bearings with the hand-bearing compass. The angles need to give a good cut when plotted on the chart. Take the three bearings quickly so the boat does not move forward too much, but not so quickly that the compass does not settle. Write down the time and the log reading at the same time as the bearings. Apply the variation before plotting.

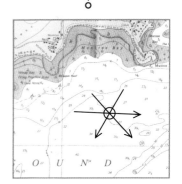

Transit and Bearing Fix

Two objects may come into line, or transit, when viewed from the boat. This can be plotted on the chart without taking the bearing or applying variation. It is quick, very accurate and only one further bearing taken at the same time will give a fix of position.

■ GPS is a very good way of getting a fix as it updates so frequently, but there are several ways it can be used, such as plotting the latitude and longitude or the distance and direction to a waypoint.

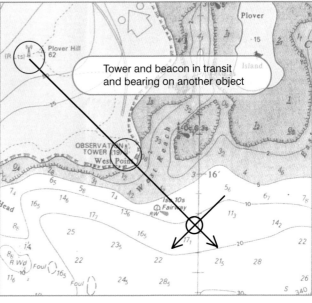

Tower and beacon in transit and bearing on another object

■ An EP, an estimated position,
can give an approximate
position if the navigator
plots the course and
distance sailed through
the water using the
information in the logbook
and then adds the tidal stream
effect at the end.

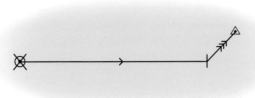

An EP can also be used to forecast
a yacht's position if it is sailing
the best course to windward
rather than the preferred course.
A predicted EP may help the
skipper decide if it will be possible to
get round a headland without tacking.

Will the boat clear the headland?

Symbols used in Chart Plotting

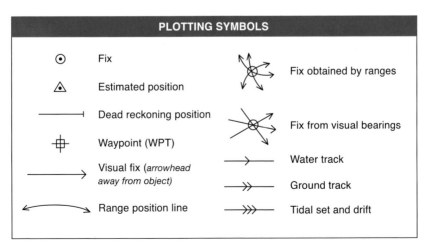

PLOTTING SYMBOLS	
⊙ Fix	Fix obtained by ranges
⬨ Estimated position	
⊢——⊣ Dead reckoning position	Fix from visual bearings
⊕ Waypoint (WPT)	
——→ Visual fix (*arrowhead away from object*)	——→ Water track
	——»— Ground track
↤——↦ Range position line	——»»— Tidal set and drift

Skippering on a Passage

Various preparations need to be done before any passage, like getting ready for any journey or holiday. Some can be done a long time in advance and then modified on the day. For example, a summer cruise could be planned over the winter with the charts and pilot books, but the boat will need to be made ready nearer the time and then the weather can change everything at the last minute.

The things to do fall into three groups and checklists can be very helpful:

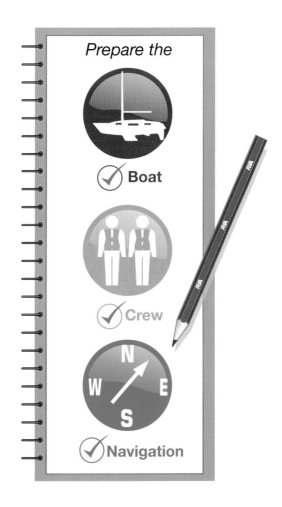

Preparing the Boat

All winter refit jobs finished and gear back on board

▤ Safety equipment serviced and expiry dates checked

▤ The VHF, instruments and navigation lights all working, including log impeller free from weed

▤ MOB equipment in position and in working order

▤ Battery operated kit such as lifebelt lights, torches, searchlight, smoke alarms all working correctly

▤ Radar reflector in position

▤ Sail covers off or unzipped and sails ready to hoist with the halyard attached, but secured so it does not flap about or go round the shroud

▤ Ensign in place

▤ All gear stowed ready for sea, on deck and down below

▤ Seacocks for heads and sink closed, if necessary

▤ All hatches shut before departure

▤ Bilges dry

▤ Daily engine checks done

▤ Water, food, fuel and gas checked

▤ Rubbish ashore

▤ Anchor ready

▤ Details of the passage, including an ETA, left with a friend ashore

▤ Weather: follow the weather patterns for a few days and get an update before sailing and during the passage. Keep an eye on the sky for weather changes and on the barometer too

▤ Consider how the forecast applies to the passage and reef in advance if it might be required

▤ In the UK, a CG66 form completed for the vessel with HM Coastguard via www.mcga.gov.uk, updated for any changes or within the last two years.

Prepare the Crew

Give a safety brief about the safety equipment, where it is and when and how to use it.

Safety Brief

- Use of a life jacket, harness and the jackstays
- How to send a VHF/DSC distress alert and Mayday
- Location and use of flares and EPIRB
- How to start the engine
- MOB equipment and procedure
- Gas safety and use of cooker
- Location and use of fire extinguishers and fire blanket. How to gain access to the engine space if there is no automatic system
- How to launch the life raft
- Location of first aid kit and manual
- The danger zones where there is a risk of injury from the mainsheet or boom in an accidental gybe

---

General Brief

- Brief the crew about the passage and delegate tasks. Don't try to do everything yourself if you are the skipper
- Check they have no medical problems and that they have medication, glasses, passports, anti-seasickness tablets, sun cream as required
- Give advice as to warm or waterproof clothing and boots for the passage. Avoid cotton materials under waterproof as cotton will retain the sweat, making people feel cold
- Use hats and sunglasses to protect against glare
- Prepare meals and snacks for the passage
- Divide the crew into watches for trips over 6 hours
- Feed the crew before departure! It can be very inconvenient to have a meal just as you set out.

Prepare the Navigation

Have the passage planned and all the data ready before leaving so the navigation during the passage does not require the skipper to spend too much time below.

Buoyage & Lights

For navigation and pilotage it is necessary to have a thorough knowledge of the buoyage system and to be able to recognise each type by day or night. IALA, the International Association of Lighthouse Authorities, regulates the navigation marks used worldwide.

The different types of buoys and beacons include:

■ **Lateral marks**

These red and green buoys and beacons are generally used to mark a channel.

The colours of these are different within IALA Region A and Region B

■ **Cardinal marks**

These are named after the cardinal points of the compass, north, south, east and west, and are used to mark a hazard

■ **Other buoys and beacons**

These include: safe watermarks, isolated danger marks, special buoys, and emergency wreck marking buoys.

IALA Region A

Red and green buoys and beacons are often called port and starboard hand marks, in Region A, because that is the side of the boat they should be when following a channel up a river or into a harbour. On charts there will be a direction of buoyage arrow to make the direction clear. If red and green buoys and beacons are lit, the lights will always be red or green, with varying characteristics.

IALA Region B

Lateral red and green buoys in Region B are the reverse in colour and colour of light, but not shape.

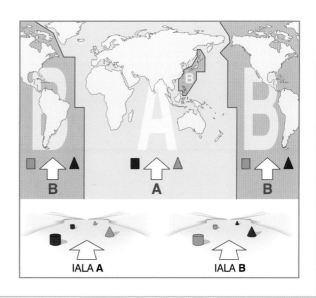

IALA A

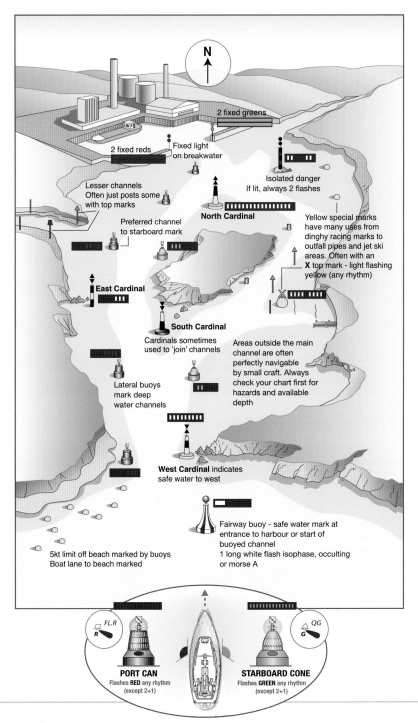

N

2 fixed greens

2 fixed reds

Fixed light on breakwater

Isolated danger
If lit, always 2 flashes

Lesser channels
Often just posts some
with top marks

North Cardinal

Yellow special marks
have many uses from
dinghy racing marks to
outfall pipes and jet ski
areas. Often with an
X top mark - light flashing
yellow (any rhythm)

Preferred channel
to starboard mark

East Cardinal

South Cardinal

Cardinals sometimes
used to 'join' channels

Areas outside the main
channel are often
perfectly navigable
by small craft. Always
check your chart first for
hazards and available
depth

Lateral buoys
mark deep
water channels

West Cardinal indicates
safe water to west

5kt limit off beach marked by buoys
Boat lane to beach marked

Fairway buoy - safe water mark at
entrance to harbour or start of
buoyed channel
1 long white flash isophase, occulting
or morse A

FL.R

R

QG

G

PORT CAN
Flashes **RED** any rhythm
(except 2+1)

STARBOARD CONE
Flashes **GREEN** any rhythm
(except 2+1)

Red and green buoys in both regions mark the channel. In major harbours and rivers there is likely to be space outside the channel for small vessels, but this is not always the case. Sometimes being just outside the marked channel will mean going aground. Check on the chart and set the echo sounder alarm.

IALA B

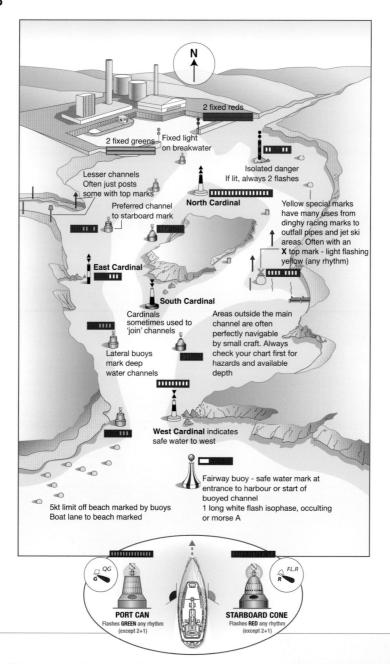

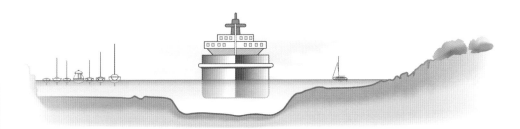

Occasionally a channel will divide so that there are two possible routes. There could be a preferred channel mark, which are red or green buoys with an opposite colour band around the middle of the buoy. These are modified lateral buoys and so differ between region A and B.

Region A Buoyage

RGR

Preferred channel to starboard

GRG

Preferred channel to port

Region B Buoyage

GRG

Preferred channel to starboard

RGR

Preferred channel to port

Cardinal Buoys

Cardinal buoys are the same within both regions and have a regular pattern of colour, topmark and light. The name shows which side of the buoy the boat should go to avoid a hazard.

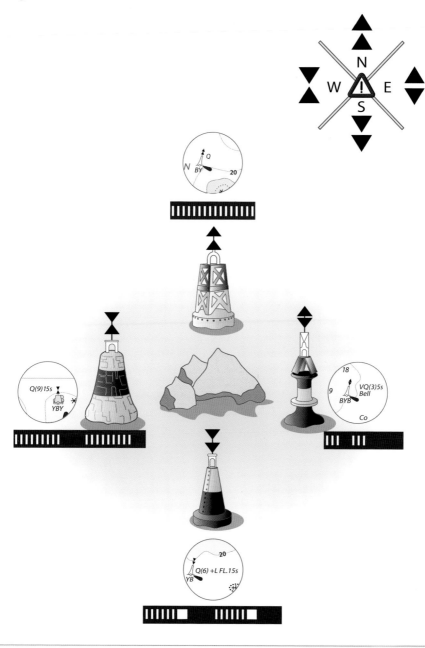

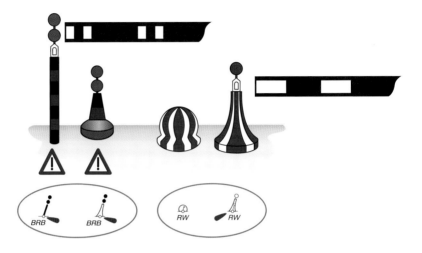

Isolated Danger Marks show the exact position of a danger

Safewater mark or fairway buoy used to show the start of a buoyed channel

RBR

Isolated Danger Mark as seen on a chart

RW

Safewater mark or fairway buoy as seen on a chart

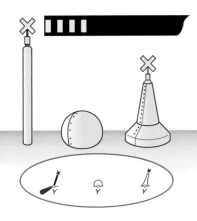

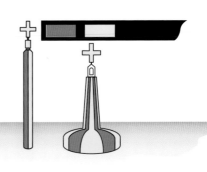

Special mark used for non-navigational reasons: racing marks, recreational areas, data collection point

Emergency Wreck Marking buoy used until permanent buoyage in place

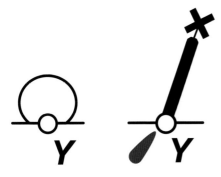

Special mark as seen on a chart

Emergency Wreck Mark as seen on a chart

Lights and Lighthouses

Lights vary in colour and characteristics. The colour is shown abbreviated to a letter, R, G, Y or Bu for red, green, yellow and blue. If no colour is shown then the light is white. The characteristic is shown as an abbreviation too.

F = Fixed

Fl. = Flashing

Fl (2) = Group flashing

Oc. = Occulting, more light than dark

Iso. = Isophase, equal periods of light and dark.

Some examples:

2 F. R. (vert)

Two fixed red lights in a vertical line, used on the end of breakwaters and jetties.

Fl. (2) G. 10s

Flashing green twice within 10 seconds. A green buoy.

Fl. (6) + L. FL. 15s

Flashing white six times followed by a long flash within 15 seconds. A south cardinal buoy.

Lighthouses and beacons show the height and range of the light.

Fl. WRG. 3s. 15m 9–6M

Flashing white red or green depending on the sectors every 3 seconds. The light is 15 metres above MHWS, mean high water springs, with a nominal range of 6 to 9 miles.

NAME	CHART SYMBOL	DESCRIPTION	VISUALLY
Fixed	F	Fixed light - always on	
Flashing	Fl	Flashing, off more than on	
Group flashing	Fl (2)	Flashing in groups	
Long flashing	LFl	Flashing, off more than on but on lasting 2 or more seconds	
Quick	Q	50 - 79 flashes per min	
Very quick	VQ	80 - 90 flashes per min	
Group quick	Q (9)	A group of quick flashes followed by a period off	
Interrupted quick	IQ	Similar to group quick but with no specified number of flashes	
Isophase	Iso	Equally on and off	
Occulting	Oc	More on than off	
Alternating	Al.WR	Colour changes	
Fixed and flashing	F Fl(2)	Fixed light with flashes at higher intensity	

Leading marks and lines are used to show the way into harbours or marinas.

Keeping the marks or lights in line keeps the boat on the safe track. When the direction is shown on the chart it will be in degrees true.

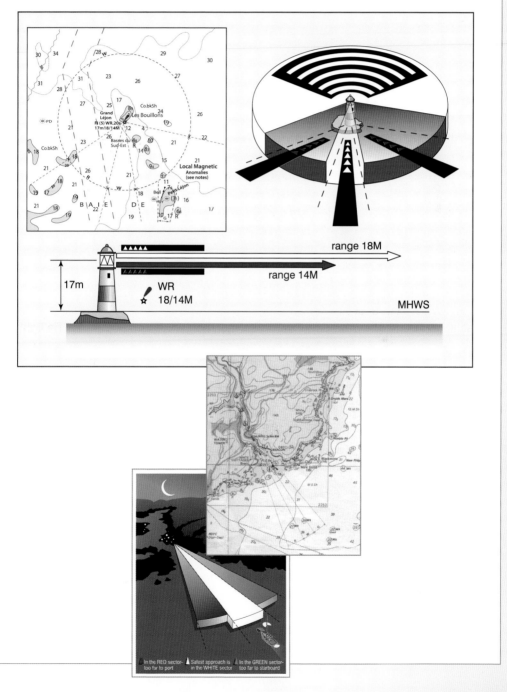

Practical Pilotage

Pilotage is the visual navigation at the beginning and end of the passage. This usually means that the boat is in an estuary, river or harbour, close to land and often other ships and boats. Decisions have to be made quickly. Arriving at an unknown port, especially at night, is challenging for any skipper and takes preparation.

In pilotage there is no time for fixes, EPs or courses to steer. Even plotting a GPS position can be too slow and keep the skipper at the chart table when it is more important to be on deck, monitoring the boat's position and looking out for navigation marks and other craft.

It is important not to forget that the tidal stream is still affecting the boat. It may be increasing or decreasing the SOG or drifting the boat off the desired heading. In daylight it is easier to judge the SOG as the boat passes buoys, moored boats or the land, but less so at night. Too little speed and the boat may drift off course; too much gives less time for decision making and may be dangerous.

In a cross-tide, monitor the course over the ground from buoy to buoy by using a compass bearing, and use the GPS to check the SOG. The echo sounder alarm will give an early warning if the boat drifts into shallow water or off a small boat route into a deep water shipping channel.

To achieve safe pilotage it is necessary to:

▨ Know the buoyage system thoroughly. All types of buoys need to be recognised quickly by their shape, colour or light characteristic

▨ Check in almanacs and pilot books for local regulations which can include:

1. Calling on or monitoring a specific VHF channel

2. Speed limits

3. A small vessel route to follow or a shipping channel to avoid

4. Traffic signals

5. A requirement for a yacht to use the engine.

Pilot books tend to give the most information and often include detailed plans and photographs, but quickly become out of date, whereas almanacs have more basic data but are updated annually.

▓ Plan the route thoroughly, including how to check that the boat is on track and where the hazards are located

▓ Calculate in advance when entry is possible. Consider the height of tide, lock or bridge opening times, darkness or any other restrictions

▓ Decide where to moor and if booking is necessary. Check for the required facilities; water, fuel, gas, repairs, chandlers or other shopping

▓ The sea conditions in the harbour entrance and the shelter at the mooring need to be considered after hearing the forecast and before starting the passage

▓ Use the hand-bearing compass, echo sounder, GPS and VHF to their full potential. Have binoculars available too

▓ Consider taking down the sails in open water and proceeding into narrow, shallow areas under power, especially if they are unfamiliar.

Some ports and harbours have leading marks and lights, transits or sectored lights to assist.

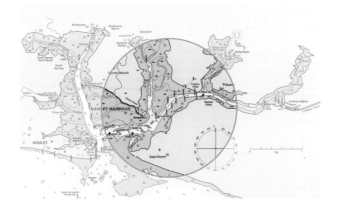

Two objects in line are said to be in transit. Leading marks and lights are provided for this, and some which occur naturally are marked on the chart.

Using transits ahead of vessel

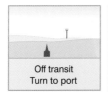

Off transit
Turn to port

On transit

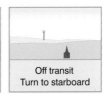

Off transit
Turn to starboard

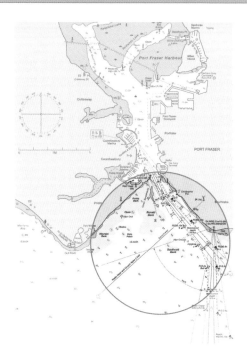

If there is no transit marked but the next buoy can be seen ahead, lining this up with the background will achieve the same result. If the background does not move relative to the buoy, the heading is correct.

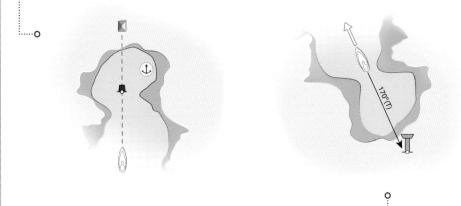

Another way to check the heading is with bearings on a prominent feature, ahead or astern of the boat. This will show if the boat is on the planned track or off track to the right or left, but not its position.

In areas where there are unseen hazards to avoid, but the boat does not want to follow a straight course, two clearing bearings can identify the safe sector.

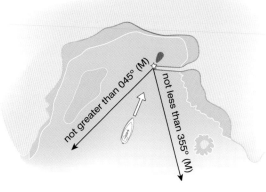

When following a channel, measure the direction and distance to the next buoy. Just turning onto the new heading may make the buoy easier to see; if it can't be seen use a back bearing to keep on course. This is especially important if there is any cross-tide.

If there is no convenient object to line up with the background or on which to take a bearing, a GPS waypoint can be used instead. The waypoint can be placed to be used like the bearing or a waypoint web can be drawn on the chart at the planning stage.

In some locations contour lines can be used as a good guide, having made allowance for the height of tide.

Once the complete plan has been made, it needs to be summarised on the chart, in a notebook or sketch map.

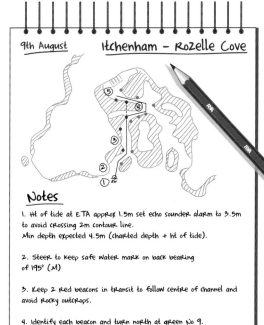

9th August   **Itchenham – Rozelle Cove**

Notes

1. Ht of tide at ETA approx 1.5m set echo sounder alarm to 3.5m to avoid crossing 2m contour line.
Min depth expected 4.5m (charted depth + ht of tide).

2. Steer to keep safe water mark on back bearing of 195° (M)

3. Keep 2 red beacons in transit to follow centre of channel and avoid rocky outcrops.

4. Identify each beacon and turn north at green No 9.

5. Call marina on ch 80 for a berth.
Prepare warps and fenders on both sides of the boat.

Weather for Sailing

Getting weather forecasts is not difficult these days. The internet offers numerous options with detailed graphics and live information, as well as the traditional shipping forecast and inshore water forecast. Once afloat, the Coastguard make regular broadcasts, as do local radio stations. In marinas, forecasts are often posted on notice boards as well. If making passages beyond VHF range a NAVTEX receiver is a good long-range alternative. All the different forecasts follow a pattern and use similar vocabulary and, to get the most value from them, practise taking notes as they are read. Write notes in a dedicated weather forecast notebook or into the ship's logbook.

The first part of the forecast will often be a description of the high and low pressure systems relevant at the time. These systems produce our weather, with the low pressure or depressions being the most significant in the UK in causing wet and windy conditions.

In the Northern Hemisphere Low pressure systems revolve anticlockwise and Highs revolve clockwise

In the Southern Hemisphere Low pressure systems revolve clockwise and Highs revolve anticlockwise

Weather Systems in the Northern Hemisphere

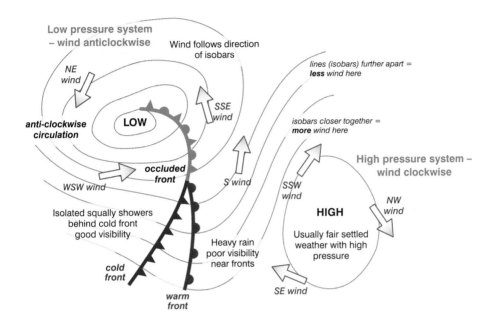

Low pressure systems or depressions approach from the Atlantic, bringing windy wet weather and sometimes producing gales and severe storms. The depth of the depression gives some indication of the severity of the weather, as does its speed of approach. The deeper and faster moving the depression, the worse the weather is likely to be. The chart above shows the isobars, which are lines of equal pressure. The closer together the isobars are on the weather chart, the stronger the wind is. The wind blows along isobars, angled slightly inwards in the case of low pressure and outwards in high pressure.

The signs of the approach of a low pressure system come a long time before the high winds and rain. High, thin, wispy cloud against a blue sky is one of the earliest signs, coming up to 12 hours ahead of the worst weather.

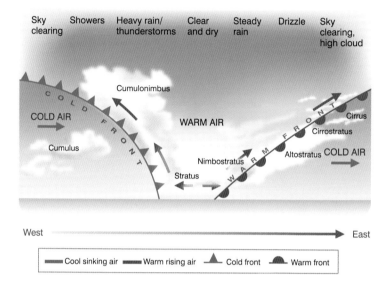

The cloud gradually becomes lower, thicker and darker as the depression gets closer, leading to a prolonged period of rain and increasing wind. This usually gives way to a period of poor visibility, perhaps with drizzle between the warm and the cold fronts. As the cold front approaches, the wind increases again, giving heavy squally rain, possibly with thunder or hail. As the low pressure system moves away there will continue to be isolated squalls with heavy rain for several hours between clearer skies, so don't expect an immediate improvement in the conditions.

High pressure systems have widely spaced isobars and usually give fair settled weather with light winds. Blue sky and puffy white clouds are common, followed by clear, sometimes chilly nights. With only light winds, sea breezes may develop and after several days poor visibility can be caused by a build up of pollution.

Weather Systems in the Southern Hemisphere

In the Southern Hemisphere the weather systems revolve in the opposite direction, and the cold fronts are particularly significant.

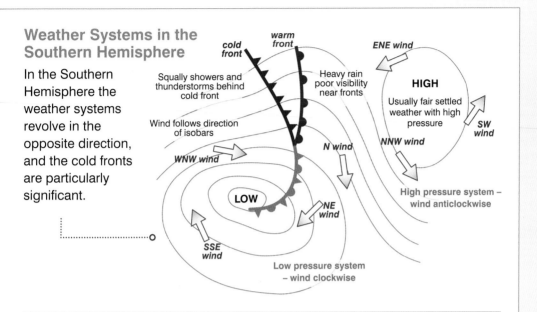

TERMS USED IN FORECASTS	
Gale Warnings	If average wind speed is expected to be F8 or more, or gusts 43–51 knots
Strong Wind Warnings	If average wind is expected to be F6 or F7. F6 is often called a 'yachtsman's gale'
Imminent	Within 6 hrs of time of issue of warning
Soon	Within 6–12 hrs of time of issue of warning
Later	More than 12 hrs from time of issue of warning
Visibility	Good – greater than 5 miles Moderate – between 2 and 5 miles Poor – 1,000m to 2 miles. Fog less than 1,000m
Fair	No significant precipitation
Backing	Wind changing in an anticlockwise direction eg: NW to SW
Veering	Wind changing in a clockwise direction eg: NE to SE
General Synopsis	How and where the weather systems are moving
Sea States	Smooth – wave height 0.2–0.5m Slight – wave height 0.5–1.25m Moderate – wave height 1.25m–2.5m Rough – wave height 2.5m–4.0m Very rough – wave height 4.0–6.0m

Beaufort Scale

1 Light airs 1–3 knots
2 Light breeze 4–6 knots

6 Strong breeze 21–27 knots
7 Near gale 28–33 knots

3 Gentle breeze 7–10 knots

8 Gale 34–40 knots
9 Severe gale 41–47 knots

4 Moderate breeze 11–16 knots
5 Fresh breeze 17–21 knots

10 Storm 48–55 knots

Sea Breezes

These local winds develop during periods of fair weather. The land warms at a faster rate than the sea, heating the air above it. This rises and is replaced by cooler air from the sea. They often occur about mid-morning and then die away later in the day. The effect is common in spring, when the sea is still cold, and the resulting wind can be up to force 4. The switch in wind direction can be quite sudden or follow a lull with no wind at all.

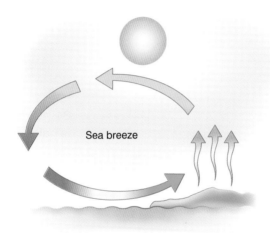

Sea breeze

On clear nights the opposite effect may occur, producing a land breeze. This is far weaker, except near mountains.

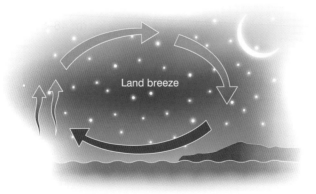

Land breeze

How does the Forecast apply to the Passage?

Obtaining weather information may be easy, but how the forecast affects the passage is what skippers have to judge when deciding to go or not. It is important not to be misled by the conditions in the marina, as the wind direction may mean it is very sheltered. Look for signs, such as trees and flags tossing about, fast-moving clouds, or boats further down the river heeling over. Even if there are no visible signs, if the forecast predicts strong wind it is best to plan for that. Reefs can be shaken out if not required, rather than put in when conditions are rough at sea by crew who are already wet, cold and cross.

Besides the wind strength, how rough conditions will be depends on four factors:

- The fetch. This is how far the wind has been blowing over the sea. This means that conditions deteriorate away from the coast if the wind is offshore. Sailing along the coast may make it possible to sail from one sheltered harbour to another protected by the land. A decision to sail downwind away from the shelter of the land will mean that the conditions get worse and worse and it will be very difficult to return to the sheltered harbour. Additionally, trying to enter a harbour in strong onshore winds can be dangerous.

- Both the direction and strength of the tidal stream in relation to the wind influence conditions. When the wind is blowing in the opposite direction to the tidal stream the conditions will be rougher, improving when the tide turns. The difference in strength between spring and neaps is influential too.

- Any swell, caused by the wind blowing in the same direction for a prolonged period, will worsen conditions. Swell can continue after the wind has dropped, making the sea conditions slow to moderate.

- The depth of water will make a difference too, with shallow water making the waves break as on a beach. This can be seen on sandbanks and other shallow areas. Breaking waves are particularly dangerous for boats. Being beam on to the breaking wave is the most hazardous.

Other factors affect how the conditions are experienced on the boat and decisions about setting out or continuing the passage. These include the size of the boat, the heading in relation to the wind direction, whether the sails are reefed appropriately and the experience and number of those on board.

Remember when planning the passage to think ahead. What will conditions be like for the return trip? When the low pressure goes through the wind will change direction, so the marina or mooring is no longer sheltered. Sailing to windward makes the wind feel stronger and is often harder work than sailing downwind. Consider too if turning back will be an option.

Fog

The definition of fog is visibility of less than 1,000m, which we most commonly experience driving home late at night or in the early hours in the autumn and winter. This gives misleading impressions, as not all fog is the same. It all reduces visibility but the reasons it has formed are varied. This may not seem important but knowing what kind of fog it is gives a better chance of predicting when it will disappear.

What we experienced driving home in autumn and winter is land fog, which forms on the long, clear nights when the heat has radiated from the ground. The air in contact with the ground is cooled and the water vapour condenses to form fog. This type of fog can be very patchy, sometimes only in low-lying areas or along roads. As the sun comes out in the morning, if the fog is thin, it will "burn off". In rivers or near the coast, land fog can also be experienced as it has drifted over the water. This may disappear as the day warms up, but on the sea the fog may be entirely different.

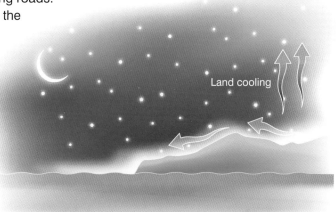

Land cooling

Generally when sailing, the fog we experience is sea fog, which is formed when warm moist air, usually from the south-west in the UK, blows over cold sea, and the moisture condenses to form fog. It is most common in spring, along the coast where the shallow water is very cold, and in summer, further out to sea where the deep water is never particularly warm. This type of fog can form when it is quite windy, and it will not burn off. If the sun shines on the top of the fog, the air is warmed and the fog may get worse. A change of wind direction, such as from south-west to north-west, so the air is no longer warmer than the sea, means the fog will cease to form.

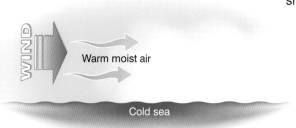

WIND

Warm moist air

Cold sea

Safety Equipment

Life Jackets, Safety Harnesses, Lines and Jackstays

A life jacket is one of the most basic bits of safety kit and there should be one for everyone on board. There are several different types available and generally they are defined by the amount of buoyancy that they provide, shown in Newtons, but also marked with EU and ISO numbers.

50N – Buoyancy Aid (EN 393 / ISO 12402-5)

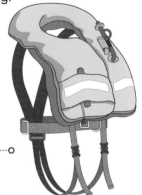

These are for good swimmers using dinghies or personal water craft, and help with floatation. They need to be worn tightly or they will ride up over the face when in the water.

100N – Basic Life jacket (EN 395 / ISO 12402-4)

This would be better for a non-swimmer than a buoyancy aid but they are not suitable for coastal and offshore cruising.

150N – Standard Life jacket (EN 356 / ISO 12402-3)

This is the standard life jacket, which is designed to turn over an unconscious person and keep their face out of the water. When packed they are comfortable and convenient to wear and all have a CO_2 bottle, manual inflation toggle, retro-reflective tape, a whistle and an oral inflation tube.

275 N (EN 399 / ISO 12402-2)

These jackets have extra buoyancy and were originally intended for offshore workers wearing heavy clothing and equipment. The additional buoyancy is good for extreme conditions but once inflated they are very restrictive.

Additional features available (ISO 12402-6):

Automatic life jackets, which inflate either when the firing head gets wet or hydrostatically from water pressure following immersion. The hydrostatic or Hammer types are less likely to fire accidentally in generally damp conditions and the cylinder is protected from corrosion because it is inside the bladder.

Harness D ring on the waist strap for a safety line. This is an excellent idea. A safety line will protect the crew from falling overboard when reefing or moving around the deck, especially in rough weather. Falling overboard puts life at risk even for a person wearing a life jacket. To be effective the safety line must be used and attachment points near the companionway are recommended so crew can clip on before coming on deck. Jackstays running along each side of the deck will enable them to remain clipped on as they move about the boat.

Lights do not come as standard on life jackets but are much better than relying on the retro-reflective tape alone. Lights are battery operated and expiry dates need to be checked.

Crotch straps. One or two crotch straps are fitted as standard on children's life jackets but not necessarily on adult jackets. The tight fit of life jackets is important to stop them riding up in the water once inflated. Crotch straps are even more effective and are less uncomfortable than an excessively tight waist strap.

Sprayhood. Sprayhoods are designed to keep the waves and spray off the face to protect the unconscious casualty from drowning. They have been proved to save lives, but need to be deployed while the person in the water is still capable of helping themselves.

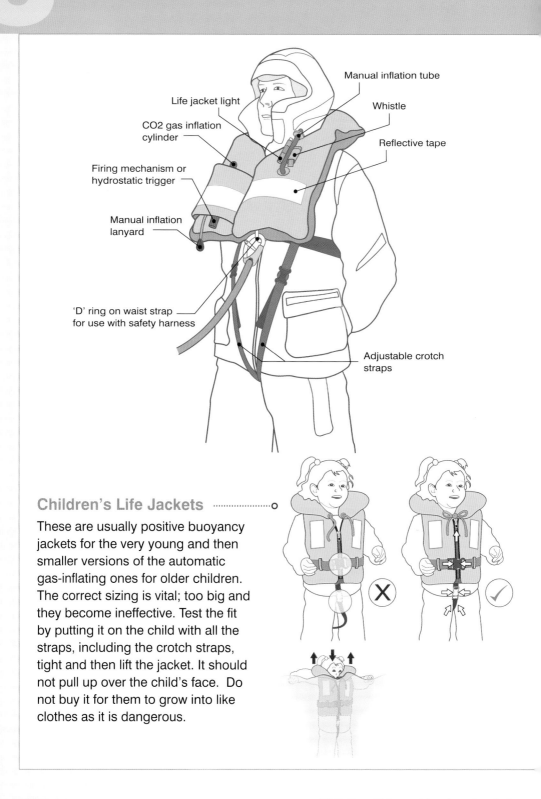

Manual inflation tube

Life jacket light

Whistle

CO2 gas inflation cylinder

Reflective tape

Firing mechanism or hydrostatic trigger

Manual inflation lanyard

'D' ring on waist strap for use with safety harness

Adjustable crotch straps

Children's Life Jackets

These are usually positive buoyancy jackets for the very young and then smaller versions of the automatic gas-inflating ones for older children. The correct sizing is vital; too big and they become ineffective. Test the fit by putting it on the child with all the straps, including the crotch straps, tight and then lift the jacket. It should not pull up over the child's face. Do not buy it for them to grow into like clothes as it is dangerous.

Fitting and Wearing Life Jackets

Number or name life jackets on the boat so that, once adjusted to fit, the crew will recognise their own. Everyone needs to know how to put it on, not to wear other clothing over the top, how to activate it manually, even if it is automatic, and most importantly when to wear it.

Generally the advice is to wear a life jacket, unless you are sure that it is safe not to. Children often wear them in marinas as well, on the boat or on the pontoons fishing!

Looking after your Life Jackets

Life jackets are important and expensive equipment, which have high levels of use and need regular checking.

Gas-inflating life jackets need inspecting regularly and servicing by an approved life jacket service agent at the manufacturer's recommended interval.

Typical Life Jacket Checks

- Check that the gas bottle is the correct size for the jacket. A 150N jacket usually uses a 33gm bottle, for example
- Check that the gas bottle is not rusty or damaged
- Check that the gas bottle is screwed in tightly or the jacket will fail to inflate
- Inflate the jacket and check for leaks
- If there is a light fitted, check that the battery is in date
- Check that the retro-reflective tape and whistle are still attached
- Check the general condition of the fabric and stitching
- Check that any additional items, such as crotch straps and spray hood, are fitted correctly
- Check there are spare bottles and auto inflation units onboard.

Man Overboard

The most important principle is, of course, do not let it happen.

A person in the water may die, even if they are wearing a life jacket. The effect of the cold may mean they will not be able to help themselves. This will make getting them back on board almost impossible, but MOB at sea is a rare occurrence and it is worth remembering that more people drown at night in marinas. Alcohol is often a factor.

Have some equipment in case of emergencies, know how to use it and practise the routines regularly. Discuss with the crew the actions that you want them to take.

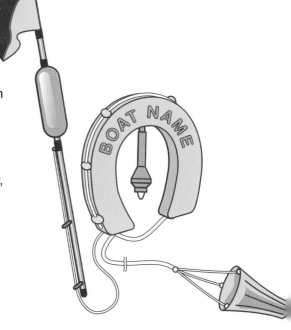

■ Lifebelts

These need to be readily available, not secured with lots of seized knotted string. Mark them with the name of the boat and fit them with a light. Check the lights regularly as some are not very reliable and collect water. Modern lifebelts are light and easy to throw, but they are carried by the wind as they are thrown and then blown across the water. This makes them hard for a person in the water to reach. Have a drogue, a small sea anchor, attached to each belt to reduce this drift.

■ Danbuoy

Once deployed, even a brightly coloured lifebelt is not that visible in big waves without the tall pole and flag of a danbuoy.

■ Other options to consider are a life sling and a throwbag, both of which can be repacked after practice drills. The life sling is rather like a soft lifebelt on a long rope, which is attached to the boat.

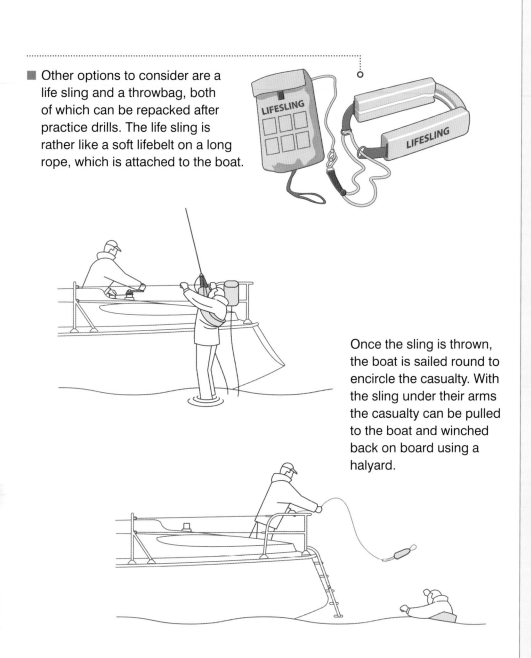

Once the sling is thrown, the boat is sailed round to encircle the casualty. With the sling under their arms the casualty can be pulled to the boat and winched back on board using a halyard.

Man overboard: Immediate actions:

SHOUT	Shout "Man overboard" to warn everybody
POINT	Nominate a crew member to point at the person in the water
THROW	Throw man overboard equipment
MAYDAY	Press the MOB button on the GPS and the distress alert button on the VHF and send a mayday

If you are shorthanded and you need to do all these actions yourself, heave to by doing a crash tack to stop the boat as near to the MOB as possible

Prepare a throwing line to secure the MOB to the boat. Crew working on the side deck should wear a safety line.

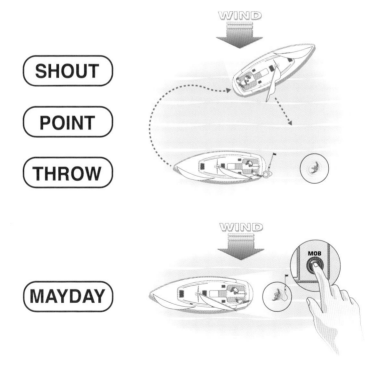

Retrieval

■ Use your engine if necessary. It would be difficult to explain why you didn't use it.

▥ Put the boat onto a beam reach and start the engine. Furl the genoa.

▥ Go about back on to a beam reach. The MOB should be ahead.

▥ Bear away onto a broad reach. Let the main go completely.

▥ Head back towards the MOB on a close reach not straight into wind. The main should be able to flap when released.

▥ Sight the MOB through the shrouds on the leeside of the boat to judge the approach. Aim to stop the boat upwind of the MOB so that it will drift down towards them.

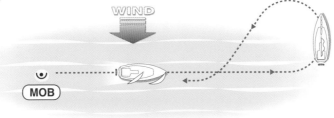

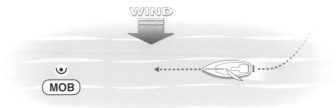

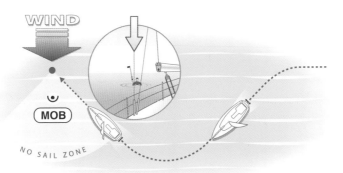

Get the casualty attached to the boat as soon as possible and get them back onboard using the stern ladder in calm conditions or a halyard winch.

The VHF radio is invaluable for receiving the weather forecast while at sea and for communicating with other boats, marinas and harbours. Consider a cockpit speaker as the radio may not be easily heard when on deck, but remember to switch off the speaker in marinas.

The boat should have a Ship Radio Licence, available free from www.ofcom.org.uk, listing all the radio transmitting equipment on the boat. In addition, at least one person on board is required to have the Short Range Radio Certificate or SRC.

Show the crew the basics when they come on board:

- How to switch the set on and select low power for routine calls
- How to change channel
- How to use the microphone
- How to send a DSC distress alert and mayday in an emergency

Put up the Mayday procedure and a list of important channels by the radio. Avoid interference to others by using the correct channel, selecting low power and not making repetitive calls. If you get no reply after a second call it's probably because you are out of range.

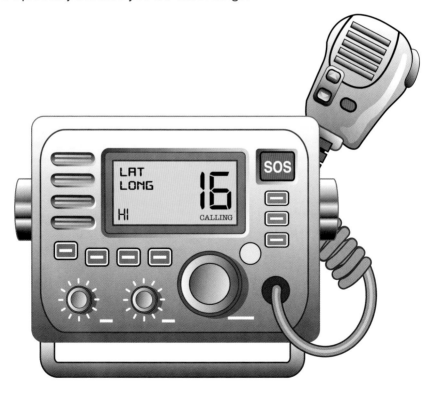

- **Channel 16.** The distress channel. Monitor this channel at sea. Use for routine calling only if there is no alternative, such as DSC or mobile phone.
- **Channels 6, 8, 72 and 77.** The inter-ship channels used to talk to other boats.
- **Channel 13.** Used by ships for bridge to bridge communication on matters of navigational safety. Useful to monitor in shipping areas.
- **Channel 67.** The channel used in the UK by HM Coastguard to talk to small craft on safety matters.
- **Channel 80.** The marina channel.
- **Local channels.** Look up the channels to call the local harbour for permission to enter or to monitor for information on shipping movements. These channels are also used for Coastguard weather forecasts in your area. Look in the almanac for these.

It is a good idea for all crew to become familiar with the use of radio.

The VHF should only be used for matters concerning the ship's business and not for chatting or making social arrangements. Use a mobile phone for that.

If you consider it necessary to do a radio check occasionally before a passage, call your marina or a friend's boat. Avoid calling the Coastguard for a radio check.

Mayday

Put your Maritime Mobile Service Identity (MMSI) number and details of your boat on a Mayday card and keep it near the radio. A mayday should only be sent if there is grave and imminent danger to vessel, vehicle, aircraft or person and the situation is life threatening.

Preceding the mayday with a DSC distress alert will sound an alarm on all DSC sets within range, including ships and at Coastguard stations. The distress alert will send the position of the boat if the set is interfaced with a GPS, eliminating one of the biggest problems for the rescue services; finding the casualty.

If it is urgent but not life threatening use a Pan Pan, or, for advice, do a routine DSC call to the Coastguard.

DSC Distress Alert

Open the red cover, then press the red button once, then press until the distress alert is sent.

During the Mayday all the communication is likely to continue on channel 16 and it will be possible to talk to the lifeboat or helicopter once they are on scene.
All vessels in the vicinity will be aware of your situation.

Do not rely on a mobile phone in an emergency at sea; it cannot perform the same functions.

MAYDAY! MAYDAY! MAYDAY!

THIS IS YACHT... yacht name spoken three times

CALL SIGN AND MMSI... give your call sign and MMSI number if DSC is fitted

MAYDAY... yacht name

CALL SIGN AND MMSI...

MY POSITION IS... give position in either lat and long or distance and bearing from a charted object

NATURE OF DISTRESS... describe in brief what the problem is, for example, sinking, MOB, boat on fire, broken down close to rocky lee shore etc

I REQUIRE IMMEDIATE ASSISTANCE

NUMBER OF PEOPLE ON BOARD... do not forget to include yourself

FURTHER INFORMATION... anything else that may help rescuers, such as abandoning to life raft, triggered EPIRB or PLB etc

OVER... the invitation to reply

Flares & other Distress Signals

There are 15 internationally recognised methods of signalling distress. Some are not very practical in this day and age, such as "flames on the foredeck, as from a burning barrel of tar" or "a gun or other explosive signal", but others need to be recognised. They are all listed in an appendix to the Collision Regulations.

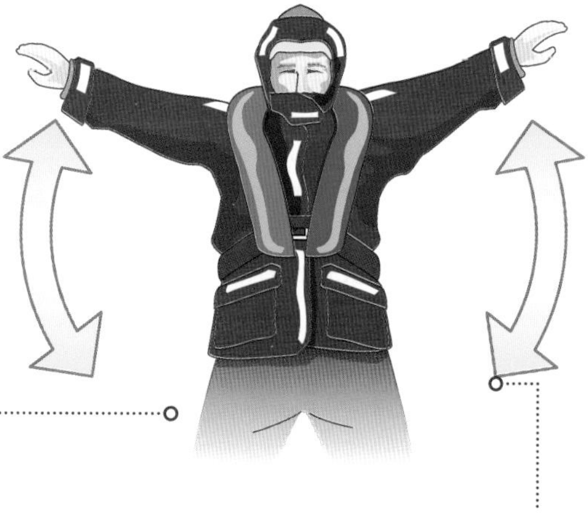

- Standing waving and lowering outstretched arms

- Code flags N over C

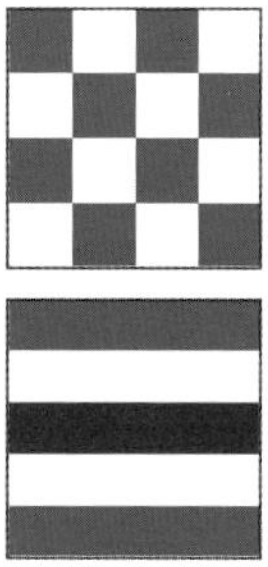

- A square flag, above or below a ball or anything resembling a ball

- Continuous sounding of the fog signal

- SOS by light or sound

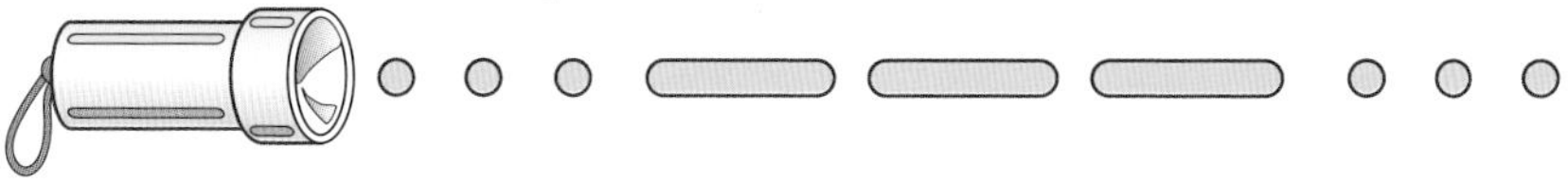

■ An EPIRB (Emergency Position Indicating Radio Beacon), operating on 406 MHz alerts the rescue services via satellites, making it a worldwide system. They are particularly recommended for vessels making passages more than 30 or 40 miles offshore, outside VHF range of the coast. EPIRBs with internal GPS give a highly accurate position and UK skippers are required to register them with the Coastguard at Falmouth at epirb@mcga.gov.uk and list them on the Ship Radio Licence as a piece of transmitting equipment.

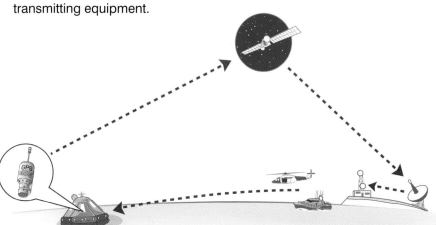

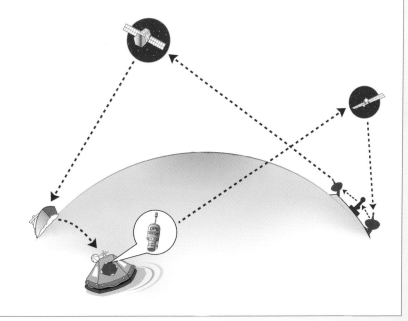

Flares & other Distress Signals

Flares, Rockets and Smoke Signals

The various types of distress signals in the flare box are for different conditions and situations. Keep the box near the cockpit, re-read the firing instructions regularly and keep a strong glove in the box too. Check for expiry dates and dispose of time expired flares safely and legally. Contact the Coastguard for advice.

Remember that it is illegal to let off distress flares, or use any other distress signal, if you are not in distress.

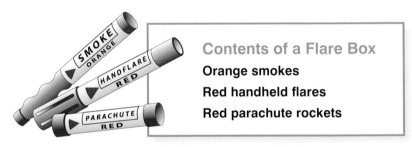

Contents of a Flare Box

Orange smokes

Red handheld flares

Red parachute rockets

The numbers recommended depend on how far from land you intend to sail.

Orange smokes can be handheld, lasting about a minute, or buoyant canisters, which last 3 or 4 minutes. Both are particularly good for signalling to helicopters, helping them to assess the wind direction. They have no illumination, making them useless at night, but are safe and easy to use as there are no flames or heat.

Red handheld flares are visible day or night, but only within 3 miles, like any handheld signal. They burn extremely hot for about a minute. Wear the glove, hold the handle and fire downwind and horizontally to protect your hand from the heat and any spitting.

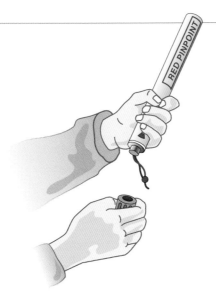

Red parachute rockets are recommended for use over 3 miles offshore because they climb to a height of 300m (1,000ft), making them visible for about 30 miles. Do not use one when there is a helicopter in the vicinity. Fire the rocket slightly downwind and let off a second within about a minute, so a bearing can be taken from another vessel.

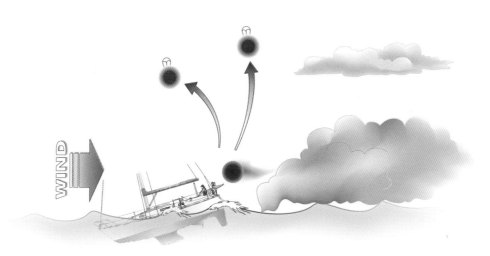

If you sight a distress smoke, flare or rocket or any other distress signal, take a bearing if possible and report the sighting to the Coastguard as soon as possible.

Emergencies with Fire and Gas

Fires are rare on boats but potentially serious. It is unlikely that outside assistance can arrive in time to give any help. Prevention is paramount.

Have fire extinguishers available in different locations on the boat, near where they might be used and near the exits. In a cabin with no hatch as an emergency exit, fit a smoke alarm as well. Dry powder extinguishers are suitable for non-liquid fires, for which AFFF foam would be better. Direct the extinguishers towards the base of the flames and, if using water to fight a fire, splash it on the flames, don't throw a bucket at a time.

Possible Causes of Fires:

- Smoking down below
- Gas build up in the bilges
- Engine overheating or fuel leaks
- Faulty wiring
- Petrol, solvent, paint, varnish and other inflammable materials stored carelessly
- Flames from the cooker setting fire to curtains, clothing or things making contact with the burners.

Have a fire blanket near, but not behind, the cooker. The fire blanket should be laid over the cooker to smother the flares, not thrown from a distance. It is important to protect your hands beneath the material if you ever have to use a fire blanket.

Types of Extinguisher

An automatic extinguisher in the engine space avoids the need to lift the hatch, introducing air and exacerbating the fire. CO2 or Halon replacement gas extinguishers are very good for this. Alternatively, have a small opening to make it possible to fire an extinguisher into the space. Check that the lagging of the engine space and hoses are up to modern standards and that there is a fuel cut-off switch outside the compartment too.

Fire extinguishers need servicing or replacing as recommended by the manufacturers. Powder extinguishers require shaking to prevent consolidation and the pressure gauge should be checked regularly too.

Safety with Gas and Cooking

Have a system for how the gas is used, and ensure everyone knows it. A good routine is to use the cut-off valve near the cooker after use and at the bottle overnight or when the boat is left empty. The gas piping, fittings and connections must be in good condition, and a qualified gas fitter can do a full safety test of the system. Gas alarms are available to detect leaks inside the boat. Fit the sensor low down, possibly in the bilges, as gas sinks, but not somewhere where it will get wet. Check that the sensor is working with a gas lighter, having blown out the flame. Don't rely on a light or alarm test when it is switched on, as this only checks the power supply to the unit.

Make sure that items left near the cooker cannot slide into the flames and catch light. Remember that the situation may alter dramatically if the boat changes direction or goes about. It is better to place the cups in the sink or on a non-slip mat and not leave the galley unattended. It is important too, that crew do not have to lean close to the flames to get to lockers or the coolbox.

The gas locker should vent to the outside. Ensure that the drain does not get blocked. Water in the locker is a sign that the drain is not working.

If, despite these precautions, you suspect a leak:

- Turn off the gas and electrics
- Open all the hatches and lift the floorboards to aid ventilation
- Don't use any flames
- Get the system checked as soon as possible.

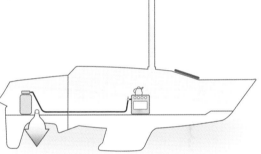

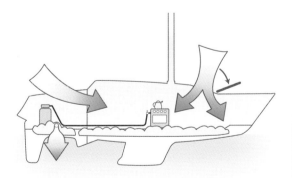

First Aid

Having a first aid box on the boat is common sense. Have a copy of the St John/ St Andrew/Red Cross First Aid Manual for reference on general first aid situations too. What should be in the box is not that dissimilar from any travel first aid kit:

First Aid Kit

- Wound dressings, triangular bandages and plasters.
- Painkillers such as paracetamol, ibuprofen, aspirin.
- Anti diarrhoea tablets.
- Antihistamine cream or tablets.
- Anti seasickness tablets.
- Sachets of rehydration mix.
- Other medicines that the crew usually need for aches and pain.
- Suncream.
- Protective gloves.
- Tufcut scissors for cutting clothing.
- Thermal protection aid, a full body survival bag.

In an emergency first aid situation, deal with the most life-threatening condition first, but:

- Get the boat under control and make the scene safe to avoid further injuries to the casualty, the crew or yourself

- Assess the casualty for their level of response. An injured or ill person who is not moving or making any noise may be unconscious and requiring immediate assistance. Ask them loudly "Are you alright?", then give a simple command "Open your eyes" or "Squeeze my hand"

- If the casualty is unresponsive open the airway and check for normal breathing.

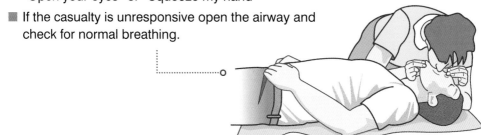

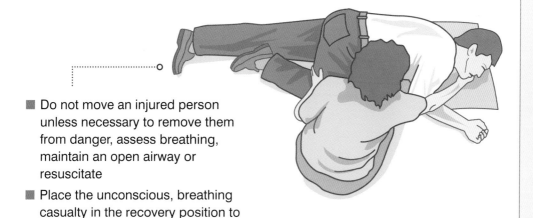

- Do not move an injured person unless necessary to remove them from danger, assess breathing, maintain an open airway or resuscitate

- Place the unconscious, breathing casualty in the recovery position to maintain an open airway

- Send a Mayday immediately if the casualty is unconscious, having difficulty breathing or has any life-threatening condition. If in doubt, call the Coastguard for medical advice. Use the VHF, not a mobile phone

- Commence CPR if the casualty is unresponsive and not breathing normally

- If in doubt about normal breathing, assume not normal. Many patients in the first few minutes following a cardiac arrest take occasional noisy gasping breaths

- If unable or unwilling to do rescue breaths, give chest compressions only, continuously at the rate of 100 per minute and only stop if they show signs of regaining consciousness and start breathing normally, or when someone else takes over

- Consider the use of a pocket mask for CPR.

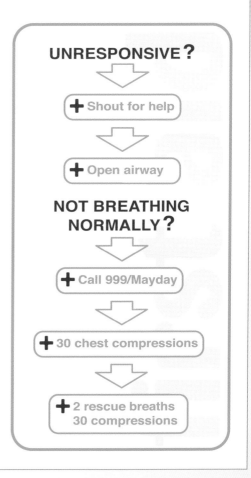

UNRESPONSIVE?

➕ Shout for help

➕ Open airway

NOT BREATHING NORMALLY?

➕ Call 999/Mayday

➕ 30 chest compressions

➕ 2 rescue breaths 30 compressions

Drowning

For a victim of drowning there is a modified CPR protocol because they have suffered a respiratory arrest, depleting the blood of oxygen, prior to the cardiac arrest.

- Give five initial breaths before starting the 30:2 CPR

- If alone, give 1 minute of CPR before going for help (www.resus.org.uk).

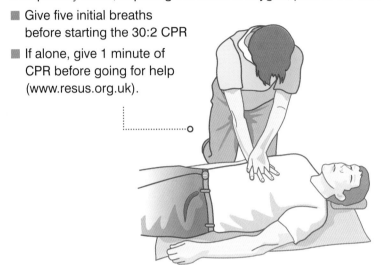

In addition to the general first aid there are some conditions of special interest to sailors. It's an uncomfortable thought that the water temperature off the UK coast can be as low as 5°C in February and rarely rises above 18°C. A substantial number of fatalities every year are caused following a sudden fall into cold water from cold shock and drowning. The majority of these deaths occur in marinas or when using a dinghy close to the shore. Hypothermia may overwhelm a casualty where rescue is delayed and can dangerously reduce the capabilities of crew exposed in a dinghy or yacht cockpit.

The initial response to immersion is cold shock. It only lasts a few minutes but the dangerous combination of rapid breathing and heart rate, cooling of the skin and pressure from the water can lead to death from cardiac arrest and stroke in susceptible individuals. In a fitter casualty, the inability to breath-hold and a phase of rapid, uncontrollable breathing may lead to the inhalation of water.

In the second phase of immersion the heart and breathing rate decrease and there begins a gradual decline of muscular strength. The ability to swim fades and hands become useless as the body temperature falls. A life jacket with a spray-hood can reduce water inhalation by 50%, but the casualty in cold water is likely to drown, not living long enough to develop hypothermia. Getting the casualty out of the water is the highest priority.

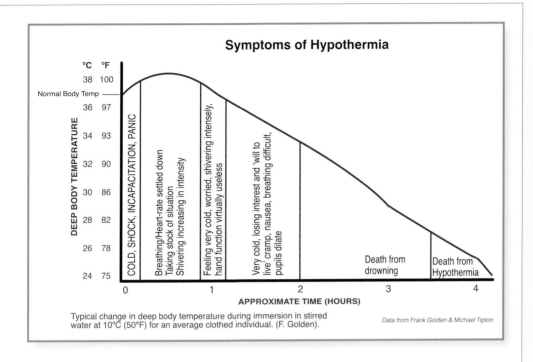

Symptoms of Hypothermia

Typical change in deep body temperature during immersion in stirred water at 10°C (50°F) for an average clothed individual. (F. Golden).

Data from Frank Golden & Michael Tipton

Hypothermia is unlikely to develop in less than 30 minutes in a fit, clothed adult if the head is out of the water. The slide into unconsciousness is gradual but, once this happens, without a sprayhood, drowning is likely as the waves wash over the face of the deeply hypothermic casualty. Even out of the water, in a life raft, the body temperature may continue to fall until cardiac arrest occurs.

After rescue, the reduction of further heat loss is vital. "Space blankets" reflect radiant body heat and are useless in this situation. A full bag-type TPA (Thermal Protection Aid), especially if it is possible to get the casualty inside, will be most effective. Insulate from any cold surface beneath the body to prevent conductive heat loss as well. The casualty needs to be treated gently and kept lying down to minimise the load on the heart.

A too-rapid rise in temperature can cause re-warming collapse.

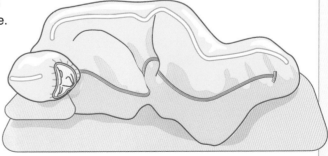

There is a history of head injuries on sailing yachts over many years and an important part of the safety brief should be the danger zones from the boom and the mainsheet. If there is a head or facial injury, assume there is a neck injury as well. Stabilise the head in the midline position if possible and, if the casualty is conscious, monitor their level of response at regular intervals. A deteriorating level of response is an important sign of a brain injury. Look for bruising, bleeding or a depression in the skull. Cover any wound and call for medical assistance on the VHF.

Seasickness is a worry for many people until they get acclimatised to the motion of the boat. About 90 per cent of sailors are affected to some degree on occasions and tablets, patches or wrist bands can help if used correctly. Time spent below (especially if reading or navigating), fumes, alcohol, fatty or spicy food, tiredness and anxiety can all make people ill. Good preparation, including passage planning, food, clothes and equipment ready and the use of watches can all help to avoid crew becoming ill. Seasickness can lead to dehydration, hypothermia, crew being careless of their safety and additional burden on others.

Sunburn, headaches from glare on the water, not drinking enough of the correct fluids, seasickness, tiredness and mild hypothermia are common at different times of the year. All reduce the performance of the skipper and crew and can be the cause of poor decisions and accidents. Hats with a brim, polarised sunglasses and suncream, together with sensible food, the correct clothing and not overly ambitious passages, can all help.

Good quality waterproof clothing and non-slip shoes are not difficult to find, but the fabrics worn underneath can make all the difference to keeping warm. Avoid cotton and choose wicking materials, like fleece, instead to get the best from breathable oilskins.

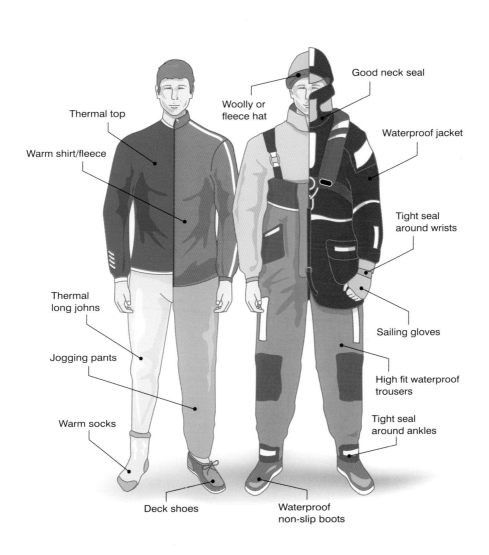

Thermal top

Warm shirt/fleece

Woolly or fleece hat

Good neck seal

Waterproof jacket

Tight seal around wrists

Thermal long johns

Jogging pants

Sailing gloves

High fit waterproof trousers

Warm socks

Tight seal around ankles

Deck shoes

Waterproof non-slip boots

Using a Life Raft

A well equipped, good quality life raft is expensive to buy and will require servicing either annually or every three years, depending on the manufacturer's recommendations, but they can be rented for a few days, a summer cruise or for the whole season.

A life raft in a valise, or soft bag, must be stored in a locker to protect it from the weather but it should be readily accessible, not buried under ropes and fenders.

A life raft in a hard GRP canister can be mounted on deck, under the boom or on the stern in a bracket. The service station needs to know if it will be lying flat, on one side or on end so that it can be packed correctly and crew should not sit on the canister, as the pressure will tend to break the seal and allow water ingress. This type of life raft can be fitted with an HRU, a hydrostatic release unit, which will automatically launch and inflate the raft if the boat sinks.

The life raft is a last resort, only to be used if there is an uncontrollable fire or the boat is sinking. In almost every other situation it is safer to remain on the boat. In a desperate emergency follow a sequence:

Preparing to launch:

- Send a mayday, activate the EPIRB and/or fire parachute rockets

- Put on warm and waterproof clothing, and life jackets

- Gather extra equipment: extra warm clothing, TPA (thermal protection aid / survival bag), sleeping bags, EPIRB, portable VHF and GPS, flare box, drinking water, food (especially carbohydrates) and first aid box

Many skippers keep this equipment in a grab bag.

Launching the raft:

- Check the painter is tied to the boat
- Launch the life raft to the leeward side, checking for debris in the water first
- Pull the painter to inflate the raft
- Put the strongest, heaviest crew member into the raft first to give it stability
- Climb into the raft, don't jump, and try to stay dry.

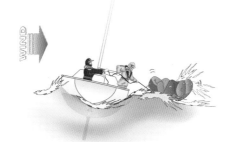

After launching:

- Cut the painter with the safety knife inside the raft by the entrance
- Stream the drogue to improve the stability and reduce the drift
- Close the door to keep out water and help keep the crew warm, but ventilate regularly
- Maintain the raft by checking for leaks and bailing out any water. Issue anti-seasickness tablets and treat any injuries. Collect any sharp objects from the crew to avoid damage to the raft. Inflate the floor.

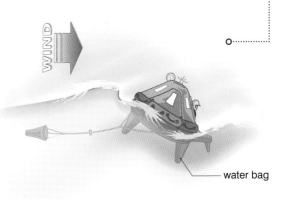

water bag

In survival situations the principles are generally the same but, outside the tropics, cold is the biggest risk and everything needs to be done to protect the crew from hypothermia. Heat loss can come from conduction through the floor of the raft or by evaporation from wet clothing, so try to prevent this. In calm conditions it may be a good idea to sit on the inflated life jackets to reduce heat loss.

Organise the crew and consider the priorities of survival.

Principles of survival:

- Protection
- Location
- Water
- Food

The RYA Sea Survival course gives the opportunity to practise life raft evacuation in a swimming pool and learn more about life rafts and the equipment they contain.

Helicopter and Lifeboat Rescue

If a helicopter is sent to your assistance it is essential to prepare the boat in good time and brief the crew before the helicopter is on scene. The noise from the helicopter is amazing. Everyone needs to know what to do in advance of its arrival, and to stay alert. The communications will generally be on channel 16 between the Coastguard, helicopter, lifeboat and the casualty vessel. If possible, it is useful to have a crew down below to monitor the VHF and pass on any instructions, which must be fully understood and followed. If you don't understand, ask for clarification.

Preparing for a helicopter:

- Put on life jackets if not already worn
- Start the engine, roll up the genoa and reef the main
- Check the deck for all loose gear, including aerials and a danbuoy attached to the pushpit, especially on the port quarter where the winchman is likely to approach the boat
- If an ill or injured person is to be evacuated, send with them details of their condition, treatment given, medications and ID.

Helicopter on scene:

- Use orange smoke in daylight or a red handheld flare in dull conditions to signal to the helicopter. Do NOT use a parachute rocket

- Listen carefully to the instructions on VHF. Once the winching has started do NOT use the radio unless something dangerous is happening

- Follow the heading and speed as directed by the pilot. It will usually be with the wind 30° on the port bow

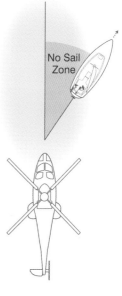

No Sail Zone

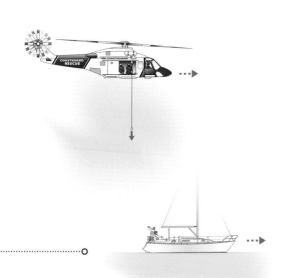

- Maintain a steady heading during the winching operation

- Allow the hi-line from the helicopter to earth in the water or on the boat before touching it to avoid a static shock

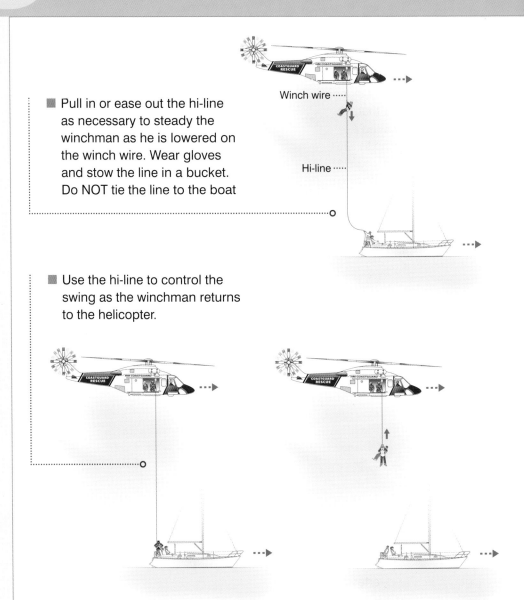

- Pull in or ease out the hi-line as necessary to steady the winchman as he is lowered on the winch wire. Wear gloves and stow the line in a bucket. Do NOT tie the line to the boat

Winch wire ·····

Hi-line ·····

- Use the hi-line to control the swing as the winchman returns to the helicopter.

Once an injured or ill crew member has been evacuated, those left onboard will need to complete the passage. Inform the Coastguard if you will need further assistance or an additional crew member.

If the lifeboat is assisting, communicate with them directly on VHF. A crewmember may be put aboard to help, or your boat may be taken under tow.

In the case of a tow, listen carefully to the instructions and consider how a tow line can be attached to your boat. A single attachment point is unlikely to be strong enough, so rig a bridle from the sheet winches on either sidedeck to the foredeck cleats. Attach the tow line to that. The tow line may be passed using a throwing line or floated down on a fender. At sea the lifeboat will use a long tow line to allow for the waves and then shorten the line when in sheltered water, or possibly change to an alongside tow. Have plenty of fenders ready for this. The best ropes to use are nylon, like the mooring and anchor warps, as they have some stretch. Sometimes a weight is used in the middle of a long tow line to reduce snatch. Check that there are no points on the line where severe chafe is possible; if there is a risk pad against it.

While being towed it is essential that the yacht is steered and follows the towing vessel. Lashing the wheel or tiller amidships will only work when the tow is long and straight.

In the case of an engine failure it may be possible, in calm conditions, for another boat or a dinghy with an outboard to assist a yacht. A fore-and-aft tow will only be possible with similar size boats. If a dinghy is used it will need to be lashed onto the quarter of the yacht and the engine run to give steerage way to the helmsman of the yacht. In good conditions it should be possible to bring the yacht alongside, but radio the marina in advance so the dinghy can be on the appropriate side for the berth. Lines will need to be rigged similar to mooring, with a bow line, stern line and springs. If two yachts tow alongside, have the bow of the towed vessel angled slightly inwards and avoid having the masts in line.

There is, unfortunately, a lot of truth in this old saying:

"There is only one thing more risky than going ashore to the pub in a dinghy, and that is coming back."

Skippers and crews sometimes forget the simple things if the dinghy is rarely used. Falling into the warm blue water of the Mediterranean or the Caribbean is very different from the cold, murky tidal waters of the UK.

- Don't overload the dinghy and risk being swamped
- Load the crew and gear into the boat evenly
- Wear a life jacket
- Climb in and out carefully
- If using an engine, take oars or a paddle as well
- Carry a small anchor
- Have the painter short enough so that, if it falls over the side, it does not go round the propeller of the outboard engine. Have a longer rope on board as well
- Take a torch at night
- Secure the dinghy carefully
- With an inflatable, take the pump
- Consider taking a portable VHF or mini-flares
- Always use a kill cord with an outboard engine
- Keep spares and other equipment in a waterproof box

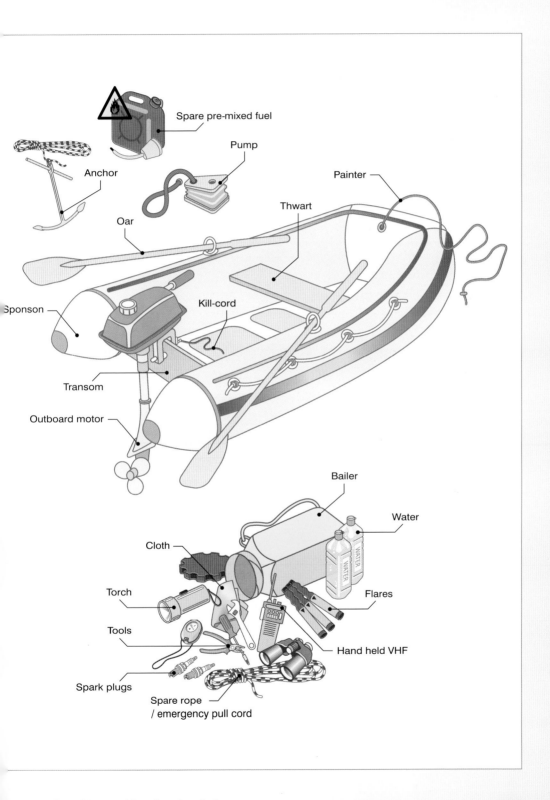

Spare pre-mixed fuel

Pump

Anchor

Painter

Oar

Thwart

Sponson

Kill-cord

Transom

Outboard motor

Bailer

Water

Cloth

Torch

Flares

Tools

Hand held VHF

Spark plugs

Spare rope
/ emergency pull cord

Monitoring the weather pattern before a passage, checking before departure and keeping up to date with any changes while on passage are all important.

The VHF broadcasts from the Coastguard are a convenient way to do this. The announcement for the routine broadcast will be made on channel 16 and will include the channel on which the forecast is to be read. If a gale warning or strong wind warning is issued it will be broadcast on receipt, preceded by a Safety Alert on VHF/DSC and/or Securité on channel 16.

If the forecast is not good or indicates the weather will deteriorate, do not make the passage at all if it will be too demanding for the skipper and crew or is unsuitable for the boat. It may be possible to set out to test the conditions and then turn back to a sheltered area. If turning back is not an option, it is probably best not to go at all, rather than risk a long arduous passage which will damage everyone's enthusiasm for future trips.

If the weather starts to deteriorate or there is a strong wind warning, get the boat and crew ready.

Strong wind warning:
- Get the crew dressed in warm waterproof clothing and boots
- Put on life jackets and issue safety lines for clipping on
- Reef the sails
- Check all the hatches are fully closed and locked
- Check the bilges are dry
- Prepare food and hot drinks
- Check the position and consider if a change of destination is advisable. Consider the sea conditions, access and shelter
- If changing to a different destination, make sure the charts are onboard
- Check the stowage
- Consider anti-seasickness tablets

Passages in thick fog are very demanding for the skipper and crew. Never set out into conditions where poor visibility makes it unsafe. Remember that not all fog will burn off as the day warms up, and, at sea, it can be windy and foggy at the same time.

If the visibility starts to deteriorate when already on a passage, consider the two dangers and do everything possible to mitigate them.

Getting Lost

This is not that likely with GPS and regular plotting, but the hazards are still there and accurate navigation is very important. Ships and other boats may be using the same waypoints, so consider a change of destination or a less busy route.

Being Run Down

The risks of being run down have not diminished with navigational aids and, if possible, avoid busy shipping areas and use AIS and radar if available.

Fog:

- Establish the position
- Consider a change of destination, away from a shipping lane or busy harbour
- Put on navigation lights
- The radar reflector should be permanently in position. If it is not, put it up immediately
- Put on life jackets if not already worn
- Make sound signals, one long blast every two minutes if motoring or one long blast followed by two short blasts if under sail
- Post extra look-outs
- Consider use of the engine
- Make for shallow water to avoid shipping routes, if safe to do so
- Make full use of all the instruments: GPS, VHF, echo sounder
- Keep to a safe speed
- Consider anchoring in a safe location
- Have white flares handy, and the dinghy or life raft ready
- Operate the radar and use AIS and radar if available.
- Wake up all the crew, especially in the forecabin

Going Aground!

After mechanical failure, going aground is still the most common reason for a call for assistance, even though almost every boat has GPS and an echo sounder. At sea, hitting rocks or a sandbank is a failure of navigation, but in rivers it can be caused by a moment of inattention or a lack of planning in the pilotage. The echo sounder alarm will give an early warning if it is set at a relatively high reading. This is especially important in areas where the shore shoals rapidly.

How dangerous it is to go aground will depend on the nature of the seabed and the weather conditions, while the chance of getting off could be determined by the tide, the quick action of the skipper and crew and the wind conditions.

Avoid the problem in unfamiliar areas by remembering:

- The inside of the bend tends to be shallow
- Two or more minor channels joining may form a split and a shallow area, so don't cut corners
- In a narrow channel with moorings, an area with no moorings may be too shallow for boats, so steering through the moorings rather than to one side can be safer
- In strong winds, keep upwind of any possible shallow areas to allow for any leeway
- If the worst happens when the boat is under sail, consider first whether the wind can help push the boat away from the shallow water, or whether it is pushing it further on.

Sail to get off weather shore

Motor to get off lee shore

■ Will heeling reduce the boat's draught? This will be the case with a fin, but not a bilge keel boat.

A fin keel has the advantage that heeling will reduce the draught, but if it is not able to get off, and if it dries out completely, it may lie right over. With a bilge keel yacht heeling will increase the draught, but the boat may be able to dry out more safely.

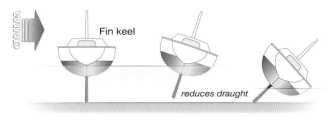

If the wind will help push the boat off, and the yacht has a fin keel, pull the sails in, encourage the boat to heel, with crew weight if necessary, and with luck the boat will refloat. Use the engine for extra power to help pivot the boat and turn it away from the shallow water.

If the wind is pushing the boat towards the shallow area let the sheets go immediately to reduce the effect. Lower the mainsail as soon as possible and furl the genoa, and use the engine in reverse.

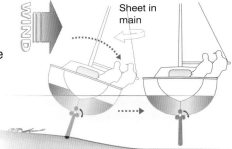

Simple Engine Problems

With servicing and proper care, diesel engines will be reliable and the daily engine checks will show any problems that are developing, but engine failure is still a cause of many RNLI call-outs. Carry the engine manual, simple spares and tools and do the RYA Diesel Engine course to help with minor problems.

Diesel Engine Servicing List

Engine manufacturers specify how their products should be maintained, particularly those units covered by extended warranty schemes. Manufacturers, dealers and the owner's handbook should have the relevant information on service procedures and intervals. However, as a general rule of thumb the following work should be carried out once a season as a minimum:

- Change engine oil and oil filter
- Check/renew sacrificial engine anodes
- Renew seawater pump impeller
- Renew air cleaner elements
- Check/adjust drive belts
- Renew crankcase breather elements (if fitted)
- Renew fuel pre-filter elements
- Renew engine fuel fine filter element
- Check/clean seawater inlet strainer
- Check gearbox/transmission oil level and quality
- Check hoses and clips
- Check anti-freeze strength. Renew if required

Generally it is a good idea, and especially over the winter, to keep the fuel tank topped up to help prevent condensation. It also helps to minimise aeration and the disturbance of any debris at the bottom of the tank in rough weather. From the fuel tank the fuel passes to the water separator with the pre-filter on top.

Any water in the fuel will be easily seen if the filter has a glass bowl and can be drained without letting air into the system. The filter being the closest to the tank is the most likely to be clogged if there is a problem with dirty fuel. Next in the system comes the fuel lift pump, which will be needed to push fuel through if it is necessary to bleed air out of the system, followed by the fine fuel filter on the side of the engine. This fine filter has a replaceable filter. The fuel then passes via the injection pump to the injectors under extremely high pressure.

Problems with the engine:

■ Turning the key and nothing happens: This is likely to be an electrical problem – no battery power to turn the starter. Few engines can be started by hand, so look for loose or damaged connections or link the domestic and engine start battery together if possible.

■ The engine turns over but will not start or will not run once the throttle is eased back: This is likely to be a fuel problem, but check first that the engine stop has been reset. Then consider the basics, such as whether there is sufficient fuel, that the fuel cut-off is switched on and that there are no signs of fuel leakage. The fuel filters might have clogged or there might be a slight air leak. Check the connections and filters, then bleed the system to remove any air in the fuel line.

How to bleed the system:

1. Open the bleed screw on the fine filter
2. Use the lift pump to push the fuel through
3. Pump until the air bubbles and froth disappear and clear fuel runs
4. Close the bleed screw.

■ No cooling water from the exhaust and/or overheating: Stop the engine and check that the water inlet seacock is open and that the strainer is not blocked. If the engine is freshwater cooled, check that there is sufficient water in the heat exchanger. Look for leaks and then check the impeller. If there are any signs of wear replace it.

How to change the impeller:

1. Turn off the seawater inlet seacock
2. Remove the plate on the front of the pump
3. Pull out the impeller taking care not to pull out the spindle as well. Check that there are no pieces missing. All of the old impeller must be removed to prevent further problems
4. Fit the new impeller held in place with the grub screw
5. Remove all of the old paper gasket before fitting the new one
6. Replace the front plate and open the seacock.

Collision Regulations

The International Regulations for the Prevention of Collisions at Sea are the law of the sea and apply to all vessels in all navigable waters connected to the sea. There may be local harbour authority rules in addition, which will be in the almanac. These may include calling on VHF for permission to enter a harbour, local speed limits or navigation channels to follow.

Some of the regulations cover general principles:

- Keep a good lookout at all times by all available means. This means watching all around, especially remembering to look astern and behind a big headsail. It is easy to be distracted from keeping a good lookout when there are other things happening on the boat such as sails being raised, reefing or preparing to enter a marina.

- Boats must proceed at a safe speed at all times. Skippers should take into account the conditions such as the visibility, density of traffic, depth, sea conditions, hazards and the manoeuvrability of their own vessel.

- Assessing the risk of collision should be done by constant bearing, not simply guesswork. The helmsman can get a similar result by lining up the approaching vessel with a stanchion, or other part of their own boat. In either case, a steady bearing means there is a risk of collision.

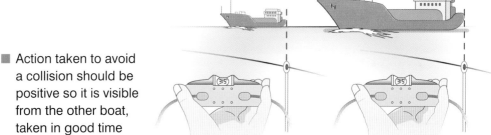

- Action taken to avoid a collision should be positive so it is visible from the other boat, taken in good time and safely done.

On the water there is no such thing as right of way. Every skipper has a duty to avoid a collision.

When there is a risk of collision, in almost every situation one boat is the "give way" vessel and the other is required to "stand on". The stand-on vessel should maintain its course and speed, unless it becomes obvious that the other boat is not giving way correctly, at which point evasive action must be taken.

The Steering and Safety Rules for Vessels within Sight of each other

There are six basic rules to learn, and it is necessary to understand the definitions used in them. The difference between a "power-driven vessel" and a "sailing vessel" may seem obvious but it is very important to remember that a yacht with the engine on becomes a power-driven vessel under the rules, irrespective of whether the sails are up.

Two power-driven vessels in a head on situation

Both boats turn to starboard to pass port to port.

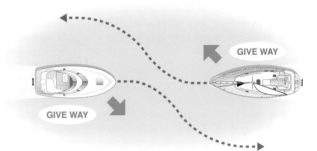

GIVE WAY

GIVE WAY

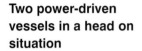

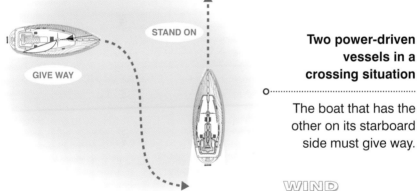

STAND ON

GIVE WAY

Two power-driven vessels in a crossing situation

The boat that has the other on its starboard side must give way.

WIND

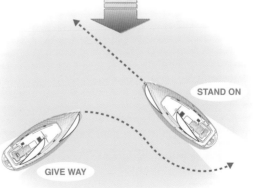

STAND ON

GIVE WAY

Two sailing boats on a different tack

The sailing vessel on the port tack must give way to the one on the starboard tack.

Collision Regulations

Two sailing boats on the same tack

The windward sailing vessel, that is the one closer to where the wind is coming from, must give way.

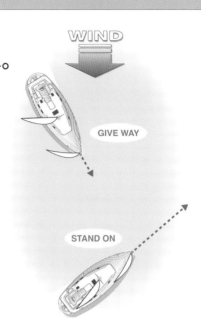

WIND

GIVE WAY

STAND ON

Power and sail

The power-driven vessel must give way to the sailing vessel.

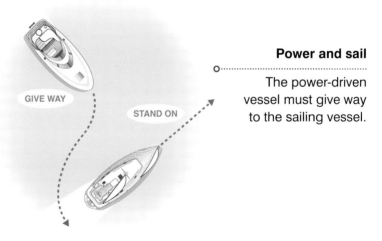

GIVE WAY

STAND ON

The overtaking rule

The overtaking vessel must give way. This rule takes precedence over other rules, such as power gives way to sail.

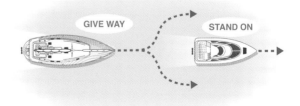

GIVE WAY

STAND ON

"Power gives way to sail" is a rule of thumb, but has several exceptions:

In a "narrow channel", yachts and small power-driven vessels must not impede a ship that has to follow the channel. They should keep to the starboard side of the channel, or even outside the channel altogether if there is sufficient depth. They should not anchor in the fairway.

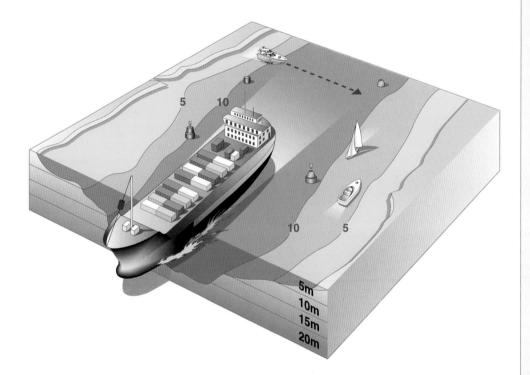

In a harbour, "Traffic Separation Schemes" and other areas where there is commercial shipping, yacht skippers must take care to avoid close-quarter situations and be aware of the limits of visibility from the bridge of a large vessel and, in some cases, their lack of manoeuvrability.

There are more complex situations when a vessel is unable to comply with the rules and has special status in the regulations. To deal with this there is an order of priority between vessels. Understanding what category vessels are in helps when learning the special lights and shapes that they show.

Order of Priority Between Vessels:

1. Vessel not under command: One that is not able to comply because of some exceptional circumstances, such as steering failure

2. Vessel restricted in its ability to manoeuvre: This is because of the nature of the work being carried out, such as dredging or surveying

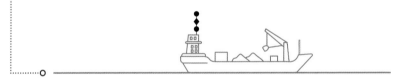

3. Vessel constrained by its draught: This is in relation to the depth of water

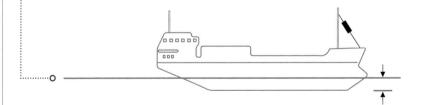

4. Vessel engaged in fishing with nets or lines so that it cannot deviate from its course

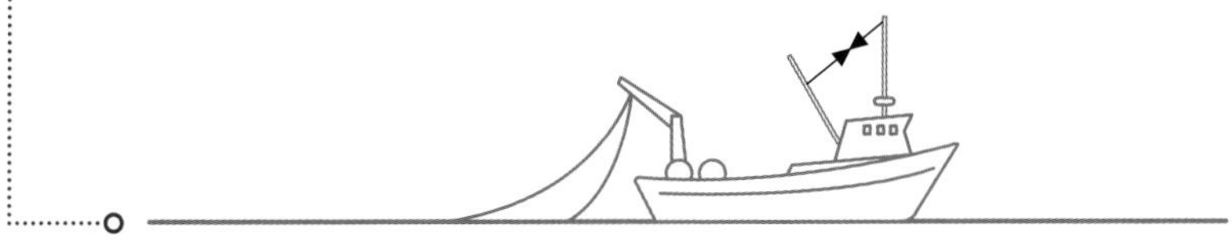

5. Sailing vessel

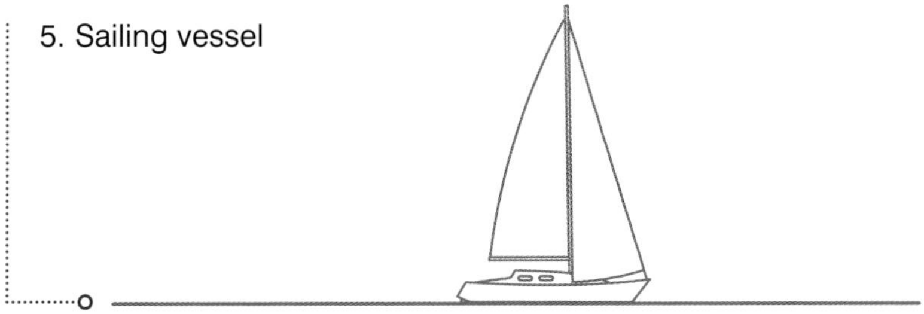

6. Power driven vessel, including a yacht using the engine with or without sails

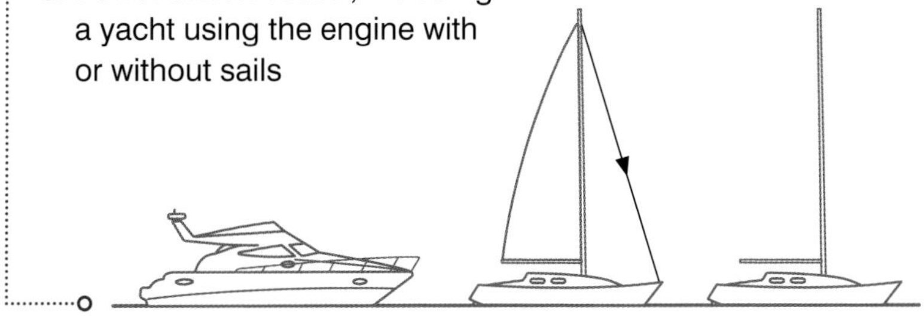

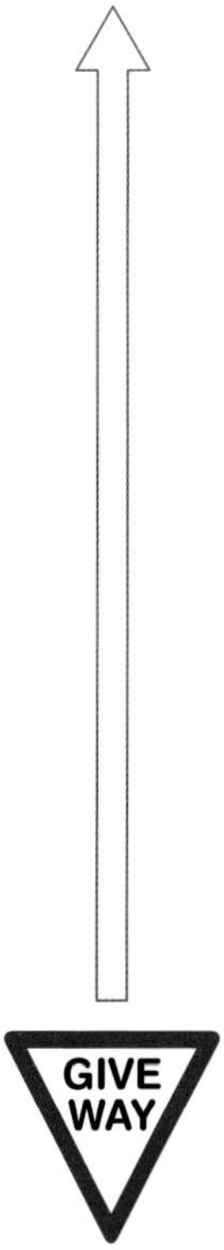

GIVE WAY

Under sail

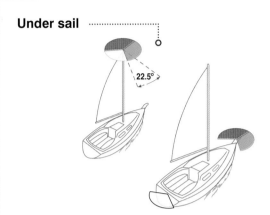

Under power

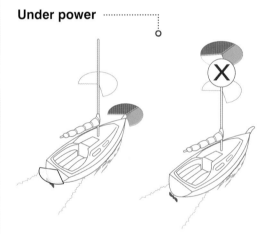

Navigation Lights

Learning just the basic lights is the way to start. Remember that the purpose of lights on boats and ships is different from on road vehicles. It is not for the helmsman to see where they are going, but for people on other boats to determine the type of vessel they are seeing and which way it is going.

A yacht needs to be capable of showing the lights for a sailing vessel and a small power-driven vessel for when the engine is being used. It is against the rules to show incorrect lights and it causes confusion for other skippers.

All vessels show red and green side lights and a stern light at the angles shown. In addition, all power-driven vessels have one or two steaming lights, depending on their length, over the combined sector of the red and green lights. This light or lights must be above the red and green.

Vessels that have special status within the rules have extra lights so the priority can be judged at night. This is similar to road vehicles, which all have headlights and rear lights so we can tell which way they are going, and emergency vehicles, which have a blue flashing light to use when responding to a 999 call.

Under Power, over 50m

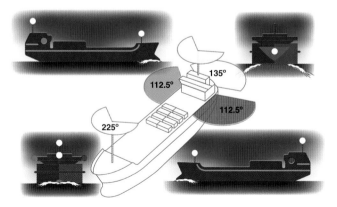

Vessels at anchor

Small vessels

Vessels over 50m

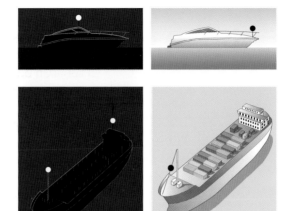

Night: Anchor light(s)   Day: Anchor ball

Other black shapes, daymarks, are used to show the special status of vessels during the day.

An important one for yachts is the motor sailing cone. A yacht with the engine on becomes a power-driven vessel under the rules, but if the sails have not been furled it may not be obvious whether the boat is motoring or sailing. It is important for other boats to know because of the collision avoidance rules. The motor sailing cone makes it clear. At night the navigation lights should be changed. Both sets should never be used as it is illegal and confusing for others.

Sound Signals

In addition to the fog signals, sound signals can be used to warn of an alteration of course or if in doubt about the intentions of another vessel.

One short blast – I am turning to starboard.

Two short blasts – I am turning to port.

Three short blasts – My engines are going astern – this does not necessarily mean the craft is going backwards.

Five or more short blasts – I don't understand your intentions – perhaps better known as "What on earth are you doing?"

Lifesaving Signals

These are the signals used by ships, aircraft or persons in distress.

Air-to-surface direct signals

Sequence of three manoeuvres meaning 'Go in this direction'. May be used to show which way to go to assist another vessel or to indicate direction to a safe haven.

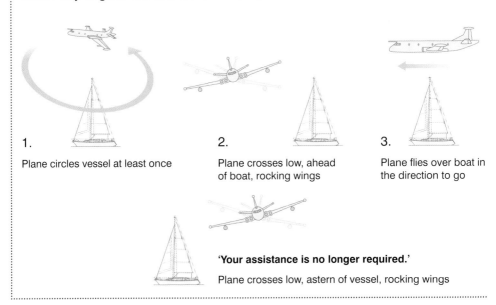

1.

Plane circles vessel at least once

2.

Plane crosses low, ahead of boat, rocking wings

3.

Plane flies over boat in the direction to go

'Your assistance is no longer required.'

Plane crosses low, astern of vessel, rocking wings

Air-to-surface replies: message understood

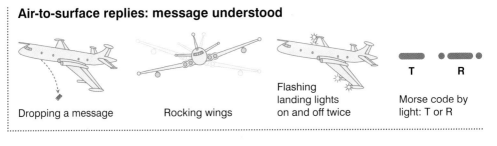

Dropping a message

Rocking wings

Flashing landing lights on and off twice

T   R

Morse code by light: T or R

Air-to-surface replies: message not understood

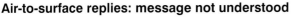

Circling

R

P

T

Straight and level flight

Morse code by light: R P T

Search and rescue unit replies

Orange smoke

Three white pocket flares

These indicate that you have been seen and assistance will be given as soon as possible.

Shore to ship signals

Safe to land here

Landing here is dangerous **with additional signals that indicate direction of safer landing place**

K

Vertical waving of arms, white flag, light or flare

Morse code letter K

Horizontal waving of light flag, light or flare

Go this way –
Put one flag or flare on the ground and move in direction of safer landing area with the other

Surface-to-air signals

  ●●● ▬ V

I require assistance

  ▬● N

No or negative

  ●▬ ▬ ▬ W

I require medical assistance

  ▬●▬● C

Yes or affirmative

Surface-to-air replies

  ▬ T

Message understood –
I will comply

Change course to required direction

Morse code (T) by light, or code and answering pennant

  ▬● N

I am unable to comply

Morse code (N) by light or code flag N.

HM Coastguard is part of the Maritime and Coastguard Agency, and has the responsibility for maritime civil search and rescue in the UK. To achieve this they maintain full-time Maritime Rescue Co-ordination Centres. These stations co-ordinate search and rescue by volunteer Coastguard Rescue teams; the RNLI; helicopters provided by the Coastguard; the Royal Navy, and the RAF and other available resources.

In the case of a Mayday within VHF range of the coast, it is the Coastguard who usually provides advice and assistance.

On a day to day basis the full-time stations also provide:

▓ Maritime Safety Information broadcasts on VHF, which include from the Meteorological Office information on gale and strong wind warnings, the inshore weather forecasts, parts of the shipping forecast, storm and tide warnings. In some areas subfacts and gunfact messages about the military activities of the MOD are provided. The local inshore forecast is particularly useful when sailing around the coast, as it is detailed and includes the outlook for the next day as well, convenient when planning a weekend or other short passage. The times of the broadcast will be in the almanac but an announcement, giving the channel on which it is broadcast, will be made on channel 16 as well.

▓ The Channel Navigation Information Service is run from Dover Coastguard and Cap Gris Nez in France. They monitor the traffic through the Dover Strait and make regular VHF information broadcasts, primarily intended for shipping. If the Coastguard see on radar a ship not following the traffic separation scheme correctly it will be identified by AIS. The ship is then contacted by VHF and directed back on course. The Dover Strait was the first traffic separation scheme in the world in what is perhaps the most congested shipping area, and monitoring these broadcasts can be interesting and provide useful information.

▓ An emergency medical information service, Medlink, is also facilitated by the Coastguard. If urgent medical information or assistance is required, call the nearest Coastguard station, prefixing the call Pan Pan. The call will be transferred to a doctor and helicopter evacuation of the casualty organised if necessary.

■ The Coastguard Voluntary Safety Identification Scheme, often known as the CG66, provides information about the boat for search and rescue purposes. This can be set up online at www.mcga.gov.uk/CG66. The information stored includes a basic description of the boat, the safety equipment carried and where the boat is normally moored and sailed, together with details of the owner and a shore contact. It is important that these details are updated every two years, or more frequently if necessary. Including a photograph of the boat is a good idea too.

■ The Coastguard is also prepared to receive a passage report. To pass the information, contact the Coastguard using a DSC routine call, remembering to include your MMSI in the first voice message for identification purposes. Only use channel 16 for calling if DSC is not available. Provide information about where the passage is from and towards, the ETA and number of persons on board. This will be recorded in the Coastguard database, which can be accessed by other stations if required. It is important that the name is recorded correctly, so be prepared to spell the name if asked, using the phonetic alphabet. Remember to call and report, at the end of the passage, either the safe arrival or any change of plans. Many skippers forget to do this and so are not using the system as intended. Forgetting to log in will not result in a full-scale search but it is useful to leave a Coastguard contact telephone number with the person on shore with whom details of the passage have also been left. The MCA guidelines suggest someone ashore should know of your passage and if this person is concerned they should contact the Coastguard. The details on the CG66 can then be used, together with any passage report, to try to locate the boat.

Index

Index

Index

Notes

RYA Training Courses

for all ages, abilities and aspirations

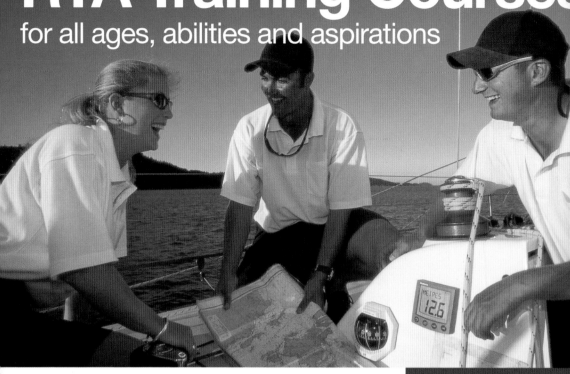

Get the most from your time on the water with our range of practical and shorebased courses.

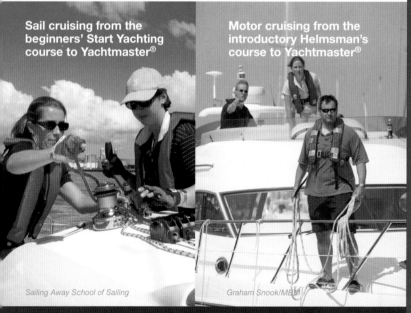

Sail cruising from the beginners' Start Yachting course to Yachtmaster®

Motor cruising from the introductory Helmsman's course to Yachtmaster®

Sailing Away School of Sailing

Graham Snook/MBM

Also, a whole range of navigation and speciali short courses:

> **ESSENTIAL NAVIGATIC AND SEAMANSHIP**

> **DAY SKIPPER**

> **COASTAL SKIPPER/ YACHTMASTER® OFFSHORE**

> **YACHTMASTER® OCE/**

> **DIESEL ENGINE**

> **OFFSHORE SAFETY**

> **VHF RADIO**

> **RADAR**

> **SEA SURVIVAL**

> **FIRST AID**

For further information see www.rya.org.uk, call 00 44 (0)23 8060 4158 for a brochure or email training@rya.org.uk

Shop online at
www.rya.org.uk/shop

- Secure online ordering

- 15% discount for RYA members

- Books, DVDs, navigation aids and lots more

- Free delivery to a UK address for RYA members on orders over £25

- Free delivery to an overseas address for RYA members on orders over £50

- Buying online from the RYA shop enables the RYA in its work on behalf of its members

www.rya.org.uk/go/join

LOVE YACHT CRUISING?

Then why not join the association that supports you?

Join the RYA today and benefit from

- Representing your interests and defending your rights of navigation
- Your International Certificate of Competence at no charge
- World leading Yachtmaster™ scheme
- Free sail numbers for Gold Members
- Personal advice and information on a wide range of cruising topics
- Legal advice on buying and selling a boat and other boating related matters
- The latest news delivered to your door or inbox by RYA magazine and e-newsletters
- Boat show privileges including an exclusive free RYA members' lounge
- Discounts on a wide range of products and services including boat insurance

Get more from your boating; support the RYA

Want to know more?

Then call our friendly and helpful membership team on 0844 556 9556 or email: member.services@rya.org.uk

The RYA... be part of it   www.rya.org.uk